C0-BWL-842

Library of
Davidson College

Memory and Understanding

Advances in Consciousness Research

Advances in Consciousness Research provides a forum for scholars from different scientific disciplines and fields of knowledge who study consciousness in its multifaceted aspects. Thus the Series will include (but not be limited to) the various areas of cognitive science, including cognitive psychology, linguistics, brain science and philosophy. The orientation of the Series is toward developing new interdisciplinary and integrative approaches for the investigation, description and theory of consciousness, as well as the practical consequences of this research for the individual and society.

Series A: Theory and Method. Contributions to the development of theory and method in the study of consciousness.

Editor

Maxim I. Stamenov
Bulgarian Academy of Sciences

Editorial Board

David Chalmers
Australian National University

Steven Macknik
Barrow Neurological Institute

Gordon G. Globus
University of California at Irvine

George Mandler
University of California at San Diego

Ray Jackendoff
Brandeis University

Susana Martinez-Conde
Barrow Neurological Institute

Christof Koch
California Institute of Technology

John R. Searle
University of California at Berkeley

Stephen Kosslyn
Harvard University

Petra Stoerig
Universität Düsseldorf

Earl Mac Cormac
Duke University

Volume 63

Memory and Understanding: Concept formation in Proust's *A la recherche du temps perdu*
by Renate Bartsch

843
P96a-xbr

0 5860 44 80

Memory and Understanding

Concept formation in Proust's
A la recherche du temps perdu

Renate Bartsch

University of Amsterdam

John Benjamins Publishing Company
Amsterdam/Philadelphia

™ The paper used in this publication meets the minimum requirements
of American National Standard for Information Sciences – Permanence
of Paper for Printed Library Materials, ANSI z39.48-1984.

Library of Congress Cataloging-in-Publication Data

Renate Bartsch
    Memory and Understanding : Concept formation in Proust's *A la recherche
       du temps perdu* / Renate Bartsch.
       p. cm. (Advances in Consciousness Research, ISSN 1381–589X ; v.
63)
    Includes bibliographical references and index.
       1. Proust, Marcel, 1871-1922. A la recherche du temps perdu. 2.
Memory in literature. I. Title. II. Series.

    PQ2631.R63A7668 2005
843'.912--dc22   2005045958
ISBN 90 272 5199 1 (Eur.) / 1 58811 643 3 (US) (Hb; alk. paper)

© 2005 – John Benjamins B.V.
No part of this book may be reproduced in any form, by print, photoprint, microfilm, or
any other means, without written permission from the publisher.

John Benjamins Publishing Co. · P.O. Box 36224 · 1020 ME Amsterdam · The Netherlands
John Benjamins North America · P.O. Box 27519 · Philadelphia PA 19118-0519 · USA

Table of contents

Preface

This study presents a theory and model of memory and remembrance, which is a further explication of the theory of Dynamic Conceptual Semantics and of the Unconscious and Conscious, which has been developed in Bartsch (1998) *Dynamic Conceptual Semantic: A Logico-Philosophical Investigation into Concept Formation and Understanding* and in Bartsch (2002) *Consciousness Emerging: The Dynamics of Perception, Imagination, Action, Memory, Thought, and Language*.

First, an introduction is given to concept formation, remembering and understanding, and it is pointed out how phenomenological data and dynamic conceptual semantics have a correspondence in neurological structures and processes, which provide the capacity to concept formation and understanding. The neurological architecture has to consist of circuit activation along connections between groups of neurons, which is capable of generating semantically directed binding of concepts in constituent structures of situational concepts and sentences, namely types of utterances representing situations. There are groups of neurons that function as conceptual indicators, which together form the general memory, and there must also be groups of neurons that function as indices for episodes, which form the basis of the specific memory. From there the constituent structure of a remembrance is constructed by connections to conceptual indicators in the general memory. When these conceptual indicators activate via their connections certain phenomenally dedicated neurons on the sensorial and motor fields, the circuit activation between the conceptual indicators on the conceptual fields with the phenomenally dedicated neurons on the sensorial and motor fields gives rise to conscious representations, being perceptions and imaginations of situations and utterances, or productions of actions and utterances. This model of memory and understanding is sketched and argued for in the first chapter and it is elaborated in the second chapter of the book.

In the second chapter, the memory of episodes and facts is presented as a capacity for construing remembrances. Remembrances are not stored as ready-made representations or images in a kind of large library or box. Rather they are generated. In order to generate remembrances with the right situational constituent structure, the specific memory must consist of groups of neurons that function as indices for specific episodes and individuals, and that direct the construction of the remembrance. It is shown in a model how the specific memory can work as a capacity for constructing remembrances by connecting from out the indices and in a structured fashion to the general memory (consisting of conceptual indicators and their inter-connections) and to emotional, sensorial, and motor fields. The specific memory works in an unconscious mode as long as the circuit activation between conceptual indicators initiated and directed by the memory indices does not involve the sensorial and motor fields. As soon as these fields are involved in the circuit activation, a conscious representation is achieved in the form of an imagination grounded in the indices of the specific memory. This then is a remembrance. Our capacity of understanding new situations consists of the working of the general and the specific memory, which makes that a new situation gets imbedded into the similarity and contiguity structures established on the whole set of our previously experienced situations in the course of building up the whole memory structure on the basis of our previous personal experiences, and possibly pre-organized to some degree by biases in the connectivity of the brain inherited and formed by mutation and selection on the basis of the experiences of individuals during the evolution of the human race. The establishment of these structures is what happens in concept formation, in ontogenesis as well as in phylogenesis. There is, thus, no difference in principle between what is learned and what is innate. These are the same kind of structures, established in history in the same way, on the basis of experienced data.

In the third chapter, the theory of concept formation and understanding, and the model of memory is related to Bergson's philosophy of memory, and it is applied to Marcel Proust's novel *A la recherche du temps perdu*, in its English translation *Remembrance of Things Past*. It is shown that, and how, Proust's novel exemplifies concept formation and understanding as based on the capacity of general and specific memory, how concept formation and remembering result in understanding new episodes based on previously experienced episodes, and how they result in the structure of the life-history explored in the consciousness of the Narrator, which is the structure of the novel. The interaction between the unconscious and the conscious, as it is explicated by more theoretical investigations of the Narrator into his life-history, are especially attended to. In this context Proust's aesthetic theorizing is analyzed in terms of the enjoyment of ones cognitive abilities, which are related to the structures of the novel. This chapter is restricted to an application of the theory of concept formation, memory, and understanding to Proust's great novel. It does not take part in the broad discussion of scholarly literature concerning the interpretation and literary criticism of Proust's work. It is merely meant to be a philosophical approach to Proust, in the light of the theory of Dynamic Conceptual Semantics and Cognitive Science.

CHAPTER 1

Introduction
Concept formation, memory, and understanding

In this introduction I present an alternative for the traditional notion of concepts and their assumed functions in descriptions and understanding. This new dynamic model of concepts and understanding, developed in Bartsch (1998, 2002), will function in developing an alternative for the traditional thinking about memory as a huge library or set of ready-made images or representations of past events. The alternative is a model of the memory as a capacity of constructing remembrances. This alternative will be formulated on two different levels of description and theorizing, firstly on the philosophical level of phenomenological data and structures on these, and secondly on the level of neurological and neuro-physiological data and theorizing. To include this second, scientific level into our philosophical considerations makes it possible to uphold a nominalist position on concepts, while at the same time being able to explain how we can understand or conceptualize new situations on the basis of previously experienced situations, and how we can employ linguistic expressions to describe these new situations, and on the other hand, how we can assign new situations to linguistic expressions as their satisfaction situations, that is "true-making" situations, on the basis of previous assignments of satisfaction situations to utterances. However, both levels, the phenomenological and the neurological, will be distinguished and not mixed up, as also Bennett and Hacker (2003) argue for. They criticize the mix-up in terminology when speaking about experiences and thoughts of people, and when speaking about their brains. I think, however, that the mix-up is not just a "mereological fallacy", where we take a part (the brain) for the whole (the person). This mix-up is mainly due to a simplistic mentalist way of identifying brain with mind, as we find it, for example, in Chomsky's writing about the "mind/brain" as a unity (among other places in Chomsky 1995). I rather argue that there is no hidden mind, but just brain and there is the expression of certain kinds of brain activity in consciousness, which is our (open) mind.

1.   On what there is not

There are no concepts. This somewhat extreme claim means that there are no mental entities, nor are there entities in the brain that are concepts. This claim agrees with the positions of Ryle, Quine, Davidson, Wittgenstein, and in some ways also with Peacocke.

Ryle, in his revolutionizing book *The Concept of Mind* (1949), argues that there is no entity that can be called the Mind; rather the Mind is a cognitive capacity or capability. It is not a place in our heads in which propositions, images and rules are stored in some medium of representation. Quine holds a nominalist position on meanings, which implies that there are no meanings of linguistic terms, rather there merely are objects as referents, and there is referring to these entities. This nominalist stance is possible by having it accompanied by a naturalistic position with respect to how reference can be achieved by language users. In his books *Word and Object* (1960) and *Roots of Reference* (1974), he elaborates the causal foundation of stimulus-meaning connected to referential use of expressions in situations, which together with the bodily states in the contexts of pre-occupations and expectations of the language user, determines what are the relevant chunks (entities and events) with which one deals in linguistic behavior and other actions. Entities are what we refer to by quantifying expressions, determiners, and pronouns. The capacity of referring by linguistic terms to entities is built up in the process of getting to know a language in its situations of use, with respect to situations that determine assent or dissent to the linguistic expressions, and thus function as situations that make us hold linguistic expressions as true or false. Quine takes observation sentences to be the linguistic expressions by which language is causally related to the world. Davidson, in his *Inquiries into Truth and Interpretation* (1985), likewise takes a nominalist's stance with respect to meanings, but he excludes the causal foundation from the philosophical discourse about language in favor of relating observation sentences to their reference situations not causally, by taking these to cause us to hold these expressions true or false, as Quine does, but by taking situations as the ones that justify us to call observation sentences, like *it is raining*, true or false, while being placed within a context of coherence with other judgments. Wittgenstein, in *Philosophische Untersuchungen* (1960, Philosophical Investigations), also excludes meanings as mental entities, and moreover he also points out that the concentration on reference as the basis of linguistic usage is much to small for explaining how language is possible. Instead he devises situations as forms of life in which language is used in kinds of language games as the foundations of language. Meaning of an expression is the use we make of the expression in situations. Being capable of using an expression correctly means to be able to extend a series of situations of use of the expression by new situations of use in such a way that others agree. This has to be learned from the old cases of use and by correction from others. The series of cases of use of an expression in principle can be continued in several ways, but some ways agree better with our feeling for regularity in the world and in action, and are (inter-subjectively) endorsed by others. The language user gets trained to make those extensions of series of use that are acceptable to the other language users from which he learns the language. Peacocke in his book *A Study of Concepts* (1992), thinks of concepts as abstract entities, what ever that might be, and proposes to analyze what it means to possess a concept instead of what a concept is. To possess a concept means to be able to find true instances of the concept, and this ability can be understood in a naturalistic way as finding certain examples compelling with respect to the concept. This finding acceptable of examples as instances of the concept is showing a disposition of a person towards realizing the conditions of possession of a concept. This disposition is something subjective, the conditions themselves are inter-subjective and objective, whereby the concept itself, the abstract entity, is objectively individuated within its instances. Thus these abstract entities are not mental entities. If we don't want to assume a platonic third realm of entities as a reality, we can think of them only as hypostasized abstractions.

The notion of a concept as a mental representation is a fiction created by philosophers, psychologists, and linguists. Locke and Hume thought that basic ideas, which were the foundation of our knowledge of the world and of our language, were formed as kind of traces or engravings in our mind by our sensorial experiences, and that all concepts were either such basic ideas or complexes composed from these. Rationalist philosophers, such as Leibniz, also assumed basic ideas, but these were thought to be inborn in the mind, and all knowledge and all concepts then were composed out of these.

The reasons that this fiction of concepts as mental representations has been upheld for so long are the following:

We try to give a rational reconstruction of our ability to conceptualize. Hereby we traditionally assume that understanding situations and understanding utterances means that we subsume certain data under certain concepts, and hereby understand, or interpret these data. Hereby we seem to need criteria for subsuming examples under a concept. Furthermore, in thinking, conceptual order, taxonomic hierarchies and semantic networks of concepts generally seem to play a role as paths along which thinking proceeds. The existence of analytic sentences is explained by assuming semantic relationships among concepts. We speak about semantic rules or meaning postulates, and a concept is the content of such a rule, in which the necessary and together sufficient criteria are spelled out for the use of the term that is understood to express the concept. The term is applicable to a situation or an object if and only if it is a realization of the concept, i.e. satisfies the criteria.

The reasons against the assumption of concepts are the following:

1. There is no clear boundary between concept and connotation: Definitions of concepts are mostly not available, and are at most approximations. It is a notorious problem in Lexicography to find a boundary between linguistic knowledge, the concept expressed by a term, and general knowledge about the instances that fall under the concept. Lexicographers are not able to provide complete definitions for lexical items, and they try to give some impression of the meaning of a term by citing example sentences, which contain the term, or they sum up sub-sorts of objects that fall under a sort that is taken to be cognitively captured by the concept expressed by the name of the sort.

2. The application of a term is vague, and so are the boundaries of its extension of application and accordingly it is not clear what features are necessary and together sufficient for forming a concept, and applying the term. There are no clear boundaries between objects that are called a mound, or a hill, or a mountain. And it depends also on the surroundings and on a norm; in a flat country, like the Netherlands, a mound or hillock is soon called a mountain. The same holds for all relative terms, like *big, long, strong*, etc., which additionally are also context-dependent in their meaning.

3. The application of a term is very context-dependent, and it changes in the history of a language. *Strong*, for example, means something quite different when said about some alcohol, some coffee, a man, an opinion, a plank, a thread, or the wind. And it is unclear whether we can call a rotten chair, which is part of an exhibition, or the chair made from fat (by the artist Josef Beuys) in the Sprengel Museum in Hannover, still a chair, since it cannot be used for sitting on; or whether we can call a rock a chair if it is very suitable for one person to sit on, when hiking in the mountains. There is no context-independent set of necessary and together sufficient set of features as conditions for the application of a term.

4. These three points are also born out by the fact that there is no fixed analytic-synthetic distinction among the general sentences we hold true. This has been argued for by Quine in his article "Two dogmas of Empiri-

cism" (1963). If there is no fixed analytic-synthetic distinction for natural language sentences, then there are also no concepts, which would be defined as sets of necessary and together sufficient conditions for the application of a term. If such concepts would exist, then there would also be an analytic-synthetic distinction in natural language, contrary to Quine's arguments. Even the standard example for an analytic sentence, namely "A bachelor is unmarried", is problematic, because the term "bachelor" can mean a Young seal in mating time, a person with the first academic degree, or an unmarried man. If one would opt out of this dilemma by assuming three different words "bachelor", expressing the three different meanings, one still would get into problems with the definition "unmarried man", because we would not call a catholic priest, who normally is not married, a bachelor, and we would not call an unmarried man who lives together with another person, especially with a woman, a bachelor; and we might call a married man, who womanizes around and is never at home with his wife, a true bachelor.

5.   We also have no consciousness of a concept; rather we are conscious merely of the examples that fall, as we say, under the same concept, by ordering them as belonging together, or by applying to them the same term.

6.   We are conscious merely of linguistic explications of a concept, which are based on explicit analyses of real and imagined examples for the use of the respective term with respect to satisfaction- (true-making) situations. These explications are only partial explications; we are not able to comprise the whole concept by such an analysis. Is there then such a whole?

7.   Furthermore, these explications of a concept by other concepts or features does not capture that the features are not loosely gathered on a heap, or gathered in a simple conjunction. Rather they are bound together in a unity, according to how they are bound together in each object or situation that is an example or an instance, or is a satisfaction situation, for the term that expresses the so-called concept. A classical concept, which is simply a conjunction of features, can not function as the type of all the examples that can be designated by the respective linguistic expression. Rather a Kantian "empirical schema", or a "gestalt", which binds the features together in the unity of an object or situation would more appropriately function as the type.

We can conclude that we have terms by which we refer to, or denote, objects and situations. Terms refer, there is reference, we can say with Quine, though there are no meanings, no concepts which the terms designate, and to which we could recourse as criteria when using the terms. This is the nominalist position. But in order to be a viable position in the philosophy of language, it still requires that there is something which makes it possible that we use the terms correctly.

2. On what there is

What there is, is understanding or conceptualizing, and herewith the ability to conceptualize. It does not consist in knowledge of or about concepts, it rather is a know-how. Everything we are aware of, including our own ways of thinking, acting, and being, is what appears to us and can thus be called phenomena or phenomenological data. They are what we experience, and could therefore also be called empirical data; and those about which two individuals agree that they both have them, can be called inter-subjective. Since the term "empirical" often is used much narrower, namely for reproducible observational data in the empirical sciences, I prefer in this context of this essay the term "phenomenological data" for all that we experience.

2.1 Phenomenological data and structures

There are *phenomenological data*; these are what we experience, and in this context especially what we experience when we learn to use a term correctly from the examples of its use given by other, competent speakers. And it is a phenomenological datum that and how we experience us as being competent speakers. We experience utterances and situations in which our model-speakers, and also ourselves, take the utterances to be satisfied, or made true.

There is *conceptualization or understanding*. This we experience ourselves and in the behavior of others. There is concept formation, namely growth of understanding. This we experience about ourselves, but also when observing children developing their language ability. There is stabilization, more or less, of concept formation. At a certain point in our development we feel competent in the use of a term: New examples of use by others fit into our own use of the term, and if not, we tend to judge these as deviant, or understand them in a metaphorical way. There are examples, and there is the linguists' and philosophers' endeavor of linguistic explication of a concept, and there is inter-subjective agreement about when something is understood and when a term is used correctly, and hereby there is agreement about conceptual analysis and explication.

There is *the role of examples and counter-examples* in the analysis or explication of concepts. There is awareness of *stabilization* of a concept or of the (relative) completeness of concept formation, namely that from some point on we feel or are aware that we learn nothing new from getting more examples about the use of a linguistic expression.

There is *stabilization* of semantic structures between lexical items (concept expressions), which we experience by taking, at some point of conceptual development, certain general sentences as analytic, or as sentences that do not express something new. And there can be destabilization when we experience something new that does not fit into the ordering structures established previously.

Although there are no concepts as mental entities, there is something we call *concept formation*, which can be described on the phenomenological level of experiences as establishing ordering structures on these experiences. In this process of ordering experiences or data, these get understood. Since the ordering structures change in the learning process, and in historical development, also our *understanding changes*, and the same realistic situation can be understood, or conceptualized, differently according to the availability of previous experiences and the ordering structures on them. Into these, the situation is placed in understanding, such that these ordering structures stay stable. The situation is embedded into a selection of ordering structures, which is due to the perspective one takes in a certain (situational) context and at a certain stage of ones life-history. This basic way of understanding will be illustrated in the last chapter of this essay.

Concept formation is based on experiences and, at the same time, it is also forming experiences as so and so aspectualized or, in other words, conceptualized. Our experiences get structured in understanding, as far as there are previous experiences with which they have similarities and contrasts, and/or with which they are associated by contiguity. Contiguity consists in different kinds of factual connectedness between objects, actions, events, situations, such as temporal, local, causal, means-ends, action-result relationships and the different roles participants play in actions. These contiguities get expressed in particular sentences, and in general sentences and theories, if they are of a general kind.

The phenomenological data that make us confident as semantically competent language users are that we are conscious of episodes and examples as falling under a concept, namely as being similar to other examples, or as being designated correctly by the respective term, and that they have factual relationships to other objects and situations. We understand situations as standing in

certain contiguity relationships with other situations. We are conscious of stability and flexibility in conceptualizing (or aspectualizing) situations, and we
are conscious of situations fitting (more or less) or non-fitting into sequences
of situations, which represent general concepts and contiguity relationships.

There is the generalizing type of concept formation by similarity under
perspectives, and at the same time, the associating type of concept formation by contiguity on the experiential level. Concept formation is ordering of
data, namely ordering of our experiences, according to contiguity and similarity under perspectives. Similarity is due to common properties in the data or
common relationships between data. Relational similarity is called *analogy*. We
realize similarity between data without knowing to which property or relationship it is due. Taking into account contiguity of experiences is an ordering of
data according to local, temporal, causal, action-participant, action-result, and
other factual relationships, which leads to associations. Analogical ordering,
that is relational similarity, presupposes recognizing contiguity.

Perspectives restrict our selection of similarity and contiguity relationships.
Without this restriction by perspectives we could not form similarity sets as the
basis of general concepts and relevant contiguity orderings, because everything
in some way or other is similar to what ever, and everything is also related,
in some way or other, to something else. Perspectives are induced by contexts
generally, by linguistic and situational contexts, and especially by desires, interests, actions, activities, habits, and by questions asked in certain situations.
Certain basic perspectives, as for example the perspective of form (which form
does x have?), or the perspective of color (of which color is x?), are innate as
similarity spaces provided within our visual system. The same holds for perspectives provided by the need to perform certain basic activities and actions,
such as drinking, eating, moving in space, etc. These activities are now additionally structured or conceptualized by culturally induced perspectives. Our
ways of life, by providing perspectives, restrict our concept formation to what
is relevant to us.

Although concepts do not exist as mental entities, we can speak of concepts as theoretical constructs primarily on the phenomenological level, and
secondarily on the level of linguistic explication. In accordance with the nominalist position, a concept can be defined in an extensional manner. This is
not done like in static semantics by the complete set of all the objects or situations to which the term is applicable. Rather a concept is seen as the result
of ongoing processes of concept formation and thus comes about by growing
sets of experienced examples or instances, especially situations of use of the respective term. The extension of a term is not directly determined by the truth

of sentences, as it is assumed in static semantics. Rather it is determined by our holding true of sentence utterances in the course of time. This is the way *Dynamic Conceptual Semantics* (DCS) (Bartsch 1998) thinks about concepts. Herein, DCS agrees with Quine rather than with Davidson. The notion of truth is, nevertheless important for correction of concept formation, since it provides a normative principle to strive at. In DCS, an experiential concept can be defined as an equivalence-class of stabilized similarity sets or series of examples, especially as an equivalence-class of similarity sets of satisfaction situations for the respective term. This is explained as follows:

Two series (similarity sets) of situations are *equivalent* if and only if the internal similarity of their union is not diminished when they are united. A person at a certain point in development has experienced a series of satisfaction situations for a linguistic expression (a full sentence utterance, a phrase, or a term). The series grows by new instances. If the addition of a new instance does not diminish the internal similarity of the set of previous instances under the relevant perspective, the set of previous instances and the new set, which includes the added example, are equivalent. Such a set of equivalent series or sets is a (quasi-)concept, established under a perspective. When it repeatedly happens that new examples added do not change the internal similarity of the growing sets of examples, we say that the quasi-concept stabilizes to become a concept. A (quasi-)concept is inter-subjective, if and only if two or more persons can add each other's examples to their own series or sets of experienced examples, without diminishing the internal similarity of their sets of experiences. This means that the different sets of examples or satisfaction situations for an expression used by different competent members of a speech community can be united. They are equivalent.

A (*quasi-*)concept expressed by an expression *e* under a certain perspective is an equivalence class of series of satisfaction-situations for utterances of *e* under this perspective.

Each member of the equivalence class is an equally good representative of the (quasi-)concept. From this follows that different people, although they have experienced different similarity sets or series of satisfaction situations for a term used under a certain perspective, they still have the same (quasi-)concept associated with that term, if and only if their similarity sets of satisfaction situations for that term can be thrown together, united, without diminishing the internal similarity measure. This means that the respective representatives of the (quasi-)concept are equivalent and experienced as equivalent in acceptability. Hereby the (quasi-)concept is inter-subjective. These people thus accept of each other their respective examples or satisfaction situations.

A *general concept* is a stabilized quasi-concept. It is equally well represented by each stabilized series of satisfaction-situations. Thus, for a person a concept is stabilized at a certain point of time, if his or her similarity set of experienced examples or satisfaction situations at this time is equivalent with the grown similarity sets at later points in time.

Stabilization of concepts means that the internal similarity of the series of examples does not diminish by adding new satisfaction situations or examples. This stabilization we experience as the fact that by new examples we do not learn anything new, compared to what we already have learned. Our concept has become stable, at least for a time. Massive data to the contrary can destabilize the concept, i.e. diminish the internal similarity, if the new data are not kept separate by being judged as deviant, or as being due to metaphorical language use.

Metaphorical use can be assumed if a perspective change is involved, such that other aspects of similarity between the previous and the new examples of use of the respective term are selected under the new, different, perspective. The new cases of use of the term are then understood as metaphorical and represent a different, new, concept, which together with the old concept forms a polysemic complex of concepts. *Polysemy* of a term thus occurs across different perspectives. This means that a term can be used differently in different contexts that establish different perspectives.

Under a single perspective concepts stand in *opposition* or contrast to each other and have to be expressed by different terms (for details cf. Bartsch 1998). Thus the term *dog* cannot be used metaphorically for a cat under the perspective of natural kind, though it could under the perspective of behavior, if the cat would show a typically doglike behavior, or would be treated like a dog, for example by leading it at a leash.

Besides general concepts we form *historical concepts*, such as partial concepts of individuals (individual concepts), events, episodes, nations, epochs, and also evolutionary lineages, and natural kinds. Historical concepts are identified by local, temporal, and causal contiguity relationships, forming the life-history of these locally and temporally connected entities; and they are characterized also by similarity relationships. An individual concept is a special kind of historical concept. It is the life-history of the individual, as we know it. It is, as such, always partial. The individual itself would be its complete life-history, into which each partial individual history will have to fit, in order for it to be true about the individual. A life-history consists of contiguous and coherent series of situations in which the individual has taken part. We shall see later in the chapter on memory that the individual must be referred to by an index located in the specific memory, or rather more precisely, in the area of the brain that is essential for organizing the capability of specific memory. This index, a group of neurons in the specific memory, established with the introduction of the individual concept into our experience and knowledge, binds together by connectivity all the indicators, likewise groups of neurons, which indicate the concepts that characterize the individual and the situations in which the individual has been a participant. A situation is likewise referred to by an index (containing a group of sub-indices) in the specific episodic memory, which binds together in a structured way the indicators that indicate the concepts aspectualizing the situation as this or that kind of situation. All this will be worked out in more detail in the chapter on memory.

Experiential general concepts and the associations between them can be explicated by theories and herewith theoretical concepts, expressed by the same name as the corresponding experiential concept, can be attached to the respective experiential concepts. Also new theoretical concepts can be created within a theory that have no direct experiential correspondence.

A *theory* is a coherent set of general sentences held true. Although on the experiential level associations based on contiguity relationships correspond with general sentences on the theoretical level, general sentences as such require reflective consciousness, because we not just have general sentences or images of situations as representations in consciousness, but also evaluate them as true or false, as probable or improbable, as safe or as doubtful. Evaluation puts a representation, which is an occurrence in our consciousness, into a reference relationship with situations outside under the point of view of fit, and into relationships with other representations (sentence inscriptions, images, or perceptions) evaluated under the point of view of coherence according to connectedness (contiguity).

Logical semantics, the semantics of the expressions *and, or, not, if-then, every, some,* modal logic of the expressions *possible, necessary,* and their deontic and epistemic counterparts, and the logic of temporal quantification are built on evaluation with respect to real and possible situations. Logical semantics therefore takes place on the level of representations, which are conscious, and it is not a matter of simple associations, which happen unconsciously or also in consciousness, but do not require reflective consciousness. The formation of theories and of logical connectedness in argumentative and narrative texts, and hereby all our theoretical concepts presuppose our ability to reflective consciousness, in which we not just live in the world and experience the world in episodic consciousness, but also consider ourselves and our beliefs and desires, especially their contents in their relationships with the world.

These contents are representations, linguistic ones and images, which we evaluate with respect to the world. In the present essay we do not treat this level of evaluative language use, which presupposes reflective consciousness with respect to first level language use. Rather we restrict ourselves to understanding situations, episodes, and basic sentences through the capacity of the general and the specific memory.

A *theoretical concept* expressed by a term *e* is the semantically characteristic syntagmatic distribution of the term within a theory, namely within a coherent set of general sentences held true. The semantically characteristic distribution of a tern *e* are all the sentential contexts of the term *e* under universal quantification, i.e. all predicates that are true together with the term under universal quantification. A theoretical concept is thus implicitly defined by a theory. It is linguistically explicated within the theory. Theoretical concepts can be ordered in semantic networks and especially taxonomies. Placed within a taxonomy, a theoretical concept becomes a formal concept. It is defined by genus proximum and differentia specifica within the taxonomic order.

Understanding on the level of theoretical concepts deals with representations by relating them to each other, evaluating them by judging their fit to external situations and by judging their fit within theories under the point of view of coherence. In the course of this essay we will not further deal with the level of theoretical concept formation, but restrict ourselves to the experiential level of concept formation and understanding.

2.2 Neurological and neuro-physiological data and structures

On the other hand, distinguished from the data and terminology of phenomenology and semantics, there are the data and the terminology of neurology and neuro-physiology about what goes on in brain and body. We assume current models for the processing of nerve stimulations and neural activity within connectionist architectures, consisting of nets of neurons and growing or strengthening connections between neurons due to activity of neurons and activity along the connections between neurons. Connections get built up and strengthened by use, whereby the synapses between dendrite and axon extensions of neurons grow stronger because they are stimulated by the activation in use. In learning processes, groups of neurons, neuronal patterns, stabilize with the input of a certain kind because of the strengthening of connections between neurons that are more and more used with this kind of input. These patterns function as more or less stable conceptual indicators, which, with a high probability, get activated from out a certain type of input, and hereby they indicate this category of input. Such conceptual, or categorical, indicators can be distributed over several neural fields; the conceptual indicator for airplanes, for example, consists at least of the indicator for the visual concept of an airplane and an indicator of the acoustic concept of an airplane, and more indicators, depending on experience and knowledge about airplanes. All these partial indicators of the concept of an airplane, the indicators of the aspects contributing to the concept of an airplane, are inter-related by connections and form together the distributed conceptual indicator of airplanes, which might be pulled together on a higher plane in the conceptual architecture by one locally concentrated indicator. We call such connected groups of neurons simply *conceptual indicators*. They get associated in learning processes with neuronal indicators for linguistic expressions. The aspectual indicators of an airplane could be directly associated with the indicator of the term *airplane*, or this can be done indirectly via a possible locally concentrated indicator, which unites the aspectual indicators into one.

By receiving input data in contiguity (related by space and time, cause-effect, action-instrument, action-result, actor-action etc.), conceptual indicators get associated to each other via strong connections and thus form relationships to each other, which mirror semantic networks. Our brain forms connectionist inter-relationships between the conceptual indicators by strengthening synapses used in proliferating activation between neurons during learning processes, which consist in experiencing the world and acquiring knowledge. The connections built up in this way are the connectionist neuronal basis of generalization, or categorization, of data to different degrees, and of association between the categories. The latter means that contiguity relationships are learned.

2.3 Correspondence between phenomenological facts and brain activity

Can a certain phenomenological fact, for example that I understand the sentence utterance *Paul hits Peter* be explained by pointing out that a certain activity of the brain (possibly visible by fMRI-scans) takes place in my brain? The answer is simply "No." Much more is necessary for that. The brain activity itself says nothing about the semantics, or the understood content, nor about the linguistic form of the utterance. Only when this brain activity, in its simplest case, is seen in (1) a history of observing my brain activities in situations of either repeated utterances of this sentence together with presented situations with respect to which I agree that Paul hits Peter, or (2) a history of observing my brain activities in situations of my agreeing to the use of the term *Peter* in situations with Peter included, *Paul* in situations with Paul included, ... *hits* ... in situations including someone hitting someone, and some proper name or noun phrase used in subject position in an active sentence in situations in which the named person performs the action indicated by the verb, and some proper name or noun phrase used in direct object position in an active sentence in which the named person is acted upon in the action indicated by the verb. By this history of observation of my linguistic or assenting behavior together with my brain activities in these situations it becomes clear that in the brain activity observed above, also the previously repeatedly observed brain activities are locally present, besides others. Hereby a correspondence can be established between understanding a certain expression, the phenomenological datum, and certain parts of brain activities. That these correspondences can be observed then can be explained by the history of my learning from other language users who *Paul* refers to, who *Peter* refers to, what *hit* means and what the syntactic form contributes to the satisfaction relationship between the sentence and the situations that make the sentence true. The locally and structurally identifiable kinds of brain activities have to be causally linked to these situations in order to have any significance for explaining why I understand the above sentence utterance. These activation patterns in my brain are indicative of the syntactic and lexical structure, and of the semantics of the sentence utterance only by these causal connections that have taken place in my learning history and that further take place in repeated experienced satisfaction situations of utterances of this sentence. In this way the kinds of brain activities, the activation patterns, are the bridges we build in learning processes from previous examples of language use to new ones. The new cases of use of expressions are causally explained from the old ones by pointing to these bridging neurological processes, the forms of which, that is the structural connections of which, have been preformed by the old cases of language use. They are the causal mediator between old and new cases of language use, which make us feel that the new case of use of a term fits into the series of old cases. The new case is understood in its linguistic form and in its semantics in such a way that it optimally fits into the series of old cases of language use. This is the causal story of explanation.

In Philosophy, one mostly is concerned not about causal explanation, but about justification. One wants to understand not why I understand the sentence utterance in a certain way, rather one wants to understand what justifies my understanding it in this or that way. I may be caused to understand a sentence in a certain way, but am I justified in this, or have I made a mistake? Explaining why this or that understanding of a sentence is right does not need recourse to causal relationships in which neurology plays a role. Here merely the relationships between old accepted cases of language use and new cases play a role. Is there inter-subjective agreement about the ways in which the new case is embedded within the structures we lay on the old data of language use, that is, can we agree that the sentence is interpreted according to syntax, morphology and lexical semantics? When we analyze what is involved in such judgments we find that finally all rests on agreement between language users about continuing series of cases of use of linguistic expressions, as Wittgenstein has pointed out. But when we go back one step more and ask on what the personal agreement, or the continuation of a series by a person is founded, we must refer to the learning history of the person within his or her social and natural setting, and what this history does to the brain of the person. From the brain, his or her agreement with the new case of use, or the continuation of the series of old cases by the new case is steered. This causal link gives rise to the feeling of fit of the new case within the series of old cases. But this feeling of fit is only right if it is in agreement with the judgment of others, and this is secured to a large degree by the social pressure under which the causal link, the bridge between old cases and new cases of use of terms in each person, was formed in learning language and its use. Therefore philosophers, as for example Davidson, put justification of language use above causal explanation. Concept formation is constraint and even induced by truth and norm, enacted by the speech community (cf. Bartsch 1998). And a philosopher like Wittgenstein points out to us where justification ends in social training, whereby the personal judgment of fit gets causally established in the learning individual and at the same time has to be permanently adjusted to social changes. The social change, especially linguistic change, we must add, comes about by individuals over-stressing the judgment of fit of the new to the old, and extending it by judging the fit of the new data within similarity and contiguity relationships under other, or new perspectives. This is the case in metaphoric language use.

Phenomenological facts, experiences and actions, correspond with neuronal events and processes, which are the mediators between previous cases of language use, perceptions and actions, and the new cases about which we feel comfortable in their fit to the old cases, and hereby feel that we understand or recognize them.

1. There is our experience of similarity and contrast of situations under certain perspectives on the phenomenological side, and there is the activation of certain groups of neurons, functioning as conceptual indicators, taking place under pre-activation of certain global fields of conceptual indicators on the neural side. The pre-activation of these fields, providing, so to

speak, pre-selected conceptual spaces, corresponds to perspectives taken, or attention spaces opened. Methodologically, the phenomenological data and structures are primary, because the corresponding conceptual indicators and structures between these can only be identified in neurological research as that what they are in their function as indicators via their correspondence with the conscious phenomenological data, our experiences and actions, and the relationships between them.

2. The similarity between data, which we experience, corresponds to the activity of conceptual indicators, which indicate members of categories due to the history of causal effects of the similar input data on the perceptive organs. A perspective, on the neural side, is a pre-selection or pre-activation of a certain field of conceptual indicators due to contexts, circumstances, desires, and actions. In other words, the conceptual spaces are opened up by contexts, circumstances, desires, and actions. The correspondence between kinds of objects and conceptual indicators is not necessarily 1-1. A category of objects that appear regularly in two very different types of contexts can have two separate conceptual indicators, due to the different contexts that have determined the input to a high degree. Hereby the objects are seen in two rather different ways. To speak with Frege, they have two "Weisen des Gegebenseins", two ways of representation. The same holds for an individual object and the corresponding partial individual concepts we have acquired of it. They can be rather different, such that they even might have, before one knows better, two different indices pointing to them in the guise of two different individual concept indicators. When one knows their identity, they get linked via the identity linking between their respective terms, or they can be linked directly, if one encounters the identity regularly in experience. The different concept indicators then get bound to a single newly introduced index for the individual.

An individual concept indicator is a network of conceptual indicators connected with an index for the individual within the specific memory basis (see below). The conceptual indicators serve to characterize the individual, when we refer to it. The individual concept indicators thus correspond to partial individual concepts, namely to (parts of) our knowledge we have about an individual. The context or situation in which reference to the individual takes place selects relevant parts of our knowledge about the individual, which corresponds to the selection of conceptual indicators in connection with the individual index.

3. We have experience of contiguity between data under perspectives: spatial, temporal, causal, and other contiguity relationships (short: contiguity-relationships) and contiguity between circumstances and the performance of actions on the phenomenological side. This contiguity corresponds with associations, connections between several conceptual indicators, including relationships between concept-indicators and habit/routine indicators (indicators for motor-activity, actions) on the neural side. The specification of the contiguity relationship can be done by circuit activation with the relation indicator (see Chapter 2, Figure 3).

4. Linguistic conceptual analysis by general sentences held true and especially by those of definitional form (i.e. theoretical and formal concepts) on the phenomenological side corresponds, as far as these general sentences are experientially based, on the neural side with activation of networks of conceptual indicators, and also with networks of linguistic term indicators. Besides this, sentences are indicated by indicators of linguistic concepts that indicate the linguistic forms of sentence representations. A theory is inscribed by a set of these linguistic indicators of general sentences held true. Conceptual analysis takes place on sentence representations and is just a conscious, mostly scientific, activity.

5. Awareness of constituent structures of phrases, especially sentences, and of situations and images, which involves binding or synthesis of parts within wholes (see below, the section on understanding) on the phenomenological side, corresponds with activation circuits between conceptual indicators and activated groups of neurons on sensorial fields/systems, on the neural side. Hereby, smaller circles are embedded within larger ones. This structure corresponds to constituent structure of situations and sentences. (The arguments for this connectionist architecture are given in Bartsch 2002.) In Chapter 2 of this essay it will also be used and extended for constructing remembrances of episodes.

3. Memory and remembering

We distinguish the general memory from the specific, or historical, memory, the latter being a memory of individual concepts (that are our concepts of individuals) and a memory of episodes and other courses of events.

The *general memory* comprises indicators of general concepts, and of routines and habits. The indicators of a general observational concept and of the corresponding routine concept of an action are linked by connections, which have been strengthened because both are mostly activated together. In learning an action we, at the same time, observe and imitate the action (on the level of motor and pre-motor activity). Likewise the connections with the indicators for objects typically participating in the action in certain roles are established and strengthened in the course of experiencing and performing the action. The group of neurons functioning as the indicator of the linguistic form concept of the word, or of the complex linguistic expression, which we use for the action, is connected, possibly via a unifying concept indicator, to both indicators, the one for the observational concept and the one for the routine concept of the action. Together these function as the concept indicator for the action.

The *historical memory* comprises indices of individual concepts, personal episodes, situations, and facts.

We now describe shortly the *kind and structure of memory*, as far as its main architecture and function is concerned.

The historical memory is the capacity of (re-) constructing partial individual concepts of individuals one has known or has information about, and the capacity of (re-) constructing previous episodes. Remembrance is an act of remembering, namely the result of this kind of (re-) construction. Memory can be seen as a collection of collections of neurons functioning as indices by means of their connections to conceptual indicators and to sensorial and motor fields, as well as to proprioceptual and emotional fields. Memory itself, as a capacity, is unconscious. It is a potentiality, a capacity or disposition to remember. Remembering an episode or person, being a result achieved by activating this capacity, is conscious. Thus, all memory, the general and the specific, is implicit. Explicit are only its products, the remembrances of individuals, episodes, and facts, and the performed acts, which are the results of activating the general memory of routines, or procedures. Also experiences of situations, perceptions, are products of the general and also the specific memory, working together with the input via the senses.

The *general memory* is materialized as a brain area or field of groups of neurons functioning as conceptual indicators and as routine indicators, with their generalizing (hierarchical) and associative connections/relationships among each other. These indicators are established over time by convergence of the impacts of learning processes in which examples are organized under perspectives by similarity and contrast, as well as by contiguity, such that, for example, the indicator for chairs is connected with those for sitting and for tables. These groups of neurons only function as conceptual indicators by virtue of their connections to other indicators, that is their position within a structure of indicators, and by virtue of the connections of the indicators to the primary fields which provide phenomenal qualities and are causally related to input from the surrounding world. These sensorial and motor, as well as the proprioceptual and the emotional and evaluative fields, provide the phenomenal material, which is the necessary medium in which conceptual structures can be couched, such that we can experience situations and objects. By their connectedness via activation circuits along connection from and to the (similarity-based) hierarchical and (contiguity-based) associative structures of conceptual and routine indicators, the activations on the primary fields become part of a conceptual ordering structure of kinds of objects, events, actions, and situations generally.

The capacity we call the general memory is not located in one compound field of neuronal indicators for objects, situations, and especially actions and routines. These groups of neurons and their interconnections by themselves are of no interest. Rather they become a functional part of a capacity only by their function as indicators, and are thus of interest to us, only by means of their connections to sensorial and motor fields, and to emotion and proprioception fields, and their relationships to the body as a functioning part within its surroundings. Only by activation taking place in circuit interaction with all this are they able to indicate anything, and are they suited to contribute to what we are conscious of, namely to our experiences. Our capacity of conceptualizing or understanding thus does not reside in a single (compounded) area; it is based on a global interaction involving conceptual fields and the sensorial-motor and other systems, the body and its surroundings. A brain cut loose from body and surrounding has no indicating, or referential function. It refers to nothing, it indicates nothing, it cannot even refer to itself because it cannot locate itself within the world, though it might live in an imaginary body, in an imaginary world, if the primary fields are still active. In such a situation, the conceptual indicators may still impose order on the activations on the primary fields, but the do not indicate objects as belonging to certain categories. The conceptual indicators are what they are only because they function together with the body in its surrounding as indicators of objects of certain categories.

The *historical, or specific, memory* is materialized as a brain area or field of groups of neurons functioning as indices (for individuals or episodes) with their connections to conceptual and routine indicators of the general memory and space-time ordering relationships, and with connections to emotion-indicators and evaluation-indicators on the respective fields. Other than an indicator, an index is not formed by a process taking place and converging over several, or even many, examples in learning across time. Rather an index is formed immediately with the experience of an episode, or with our acquaintance with an individual, or with the narrative creation of a historical entity. It must be possible to extend the index by associating sub-indices in the course of learning more about the individual or situation. An index for an individual may get connected with other indices of individuals and of episodes. Thus, an index can become more complex.

If we remember a past episode, the memory index of the past situation works just like an index for an individual. The constituent structure of activation circuits involving conceptual indicators is organized from out that index, which in itself then must be composed out of sub-indices. The constituent structure built up by activation circuits corresponds to the constituent structure of Binding-intersections between the respective concepts that characterize a situation (see for this Binding-notion the following section on *Understanding*). For a remembrance to occur, these activation circuits must include groups of neurons on sensorial and motor fields. Without phenomenal material emerging from these fields, the process of re-construction of a remembrance of an episode or of and individual would not have a remembrance as a conscious result. Rather it would stay on the conceptual fields and from there it could influence perception and action, but that activity would remain unconscious for us. In such a case we cannot compare the new perception with the past episode, though the past episode has influence on our understanding of the new situation.

In a remembrance of an episode, the activation circuits form a whole of smaller and larger circuits that also include neurons on the sensorial, motor, emotional, and proprioceptual fields, whereby neurons dedicated to phenomenal expression provide phenomenal material ('qualia') necessary for a conceptually structured episode emerging in consciousness. Argumentation for such a structure of activation circuits is based on the structural requirements of a dynamic conceptual semantics, as it can be found in Bartsch (2002). On the other hand, there is evidence and argumentation from neuro-psychological research by Lamme and Roelfsema (2000) and Lamme (2002), who claim that consciousness emerges only when recurrent activation between higher and lower areas occurs. Simple feed-forward activation presents information processing but does not result in conscious awareness. Also Miyashita (2004) reports about research done into the circuit activation, on a fine-grained level of molecular and cellular physiological processes and anatomical growth resulting in morphological change, between the major subfields of the hippocampus and between the hippocampus and cortical fields in the frontal and temporal lobe, done in the context of memory consolidation and in retrieval, whereby memory consolidation amounts to a structural reorganization of neural circuits. The research reviewed by Miyashita (2004) has been done in mice, rats, monkeys and humans.

The specific memory field, which contains episodic and individual indices, is closely connected with emotional, proprioceptual, sensorial and routine and motor fields, from where memories of episodes can be induced, besides from indicators of general concepts. In principle, memories are constructed by the connectivity that had been established by the similarities and associations between previous data. The similarities and contiguities leading to associations were selected under certain perspectives, which correspond to certain pre-activations, contextually and situationally induced. We see that the specific memory is not located in one single field, identified by neurologists as the hippocampus. Rather the capacity of memory is based on a global interaction between the field of memory indices, the hippocampus, and the other fields presented in the architecture below in Chapter 2.1.

We have assumed that both kinds of memory, the general memory and the specific memory, have connections with the sensorial, motor, emotional, evaluative, and proprioceptional areas. By interaction circuits between indicators in these areas and indices in the historical memory we perceive and imagine episodes (linguistic as well as situational ones) and perceive, imagine, and recognize individuals.

4. Understanding

We distinguish understanding a situation from understanding a linguistic expression, although both make use of the same principles and structures on the phenomenological level and, correspondingly, on the level of connectionist neural architecture.

(1) *Understanding a situation* is conceptualizing the situation, by which aspects are distinguished within the situation. We therefore also speak of aspectualizing a situation. We can say that the situation is embedded into the conceptual system, the ordering established on our set of experienced situations, at this point in the development of concept formation in a person's history of learning. The embedding happens under preservation of stability of the conceptual system. What does that mean?

Above, an experiential general concept was defined as an equivalence-class of stabilizing series of examples that are similarity sets under a certain perspective, or under a group of perspectives. Two similarity sets were called equivalent if and only if they can be united (thrown together) without changing the internal similarity measure. That is, the two sets do not add anything to each other as far as the concept is concerned. They both represent the concept equally well, as also does their union. If the internal similarity measure of a set of examples, namely satisfaction situations for an expression e, does not change anymore by adding new examples or satisfaction-situations, then this growing set of examples is stable at that point and, for now, completely represents the concept, which itself is the whole equivalence class, expressed by e. A situation can be understood, which means can be aspectualized or conceptualized under that concept, if and only if the situation can be added to, or fitted into, a similarity set representing the concept. This means that the situation can be added to a representative similarity set of previous experiences without diminishing its internal similarity measure, which thus remains stable. In this way, we understand a situation if and only if the situation is integrated into our concept representing set of examples 'salva stabilitate'. If we inter-subjectively entertain the same concept, that is if our concept representing similarity sets are equivalent, then the situation can be said to be embeddable into our inter-subjective concept salva stabilitate. Then we understand the situation in the same way, at least as far as this conceptualization goes.

Understanding a situation as one in which a certain individual is involved as a participant, for example as agent, means that the situation is embeddable into the partial individual concept (the representation, that is the partial life-history of the individual we have knowledge of) under preservation of coherence between the situations that define the partial life-history of the individual as we know it. To understand, for example, John as an agent in a situation means that we find there within a smallest situation the individual concept of John and the general concept of an agent bound together in a constituent, and bound together with some action concept, for example the concept of eating. This means that the situation contains a smallest situation, which

1. fits into the individual concept of John, a coherent series of situations of John's life-history as we know it, and which
2. fits into the general concept of an agent, namely into a similarity set of situations in which someone is an agent, and which
3. fits into the general concept of eating, a similarity set of eat-situations.

Understanding a situation thus consists in adding it to, or integrating it into, the conceptual representations we have, namely into the series of previous examples of a general concept, or into a series of experienced or known occurrences of an individual, under preservation of their stability and/or coherence.

Understanding a situation that in some respect does not fit into our conceptual system is possible by *metaphorical understanding*. This is also understanding by similarity, but now under a new perspective, which makes it possible to continue a series of examples for a term *e* in a new way, due to similarities that are selected under this new perspective. Hereby we form a new concept expressed by *e* under another perspective, or another type of contexts, than the perspective that was relevant for the previous uses of the expression. A problematic situation, in which, for example, a man is called a snail, fits into the series of uses of *snail* under the new perspective and is now understood as, for example, a situation containing someone that can be called a snail under the perspective of behavior, especially with respect to his way of showing motor activity, rather than under the perspective of natural kind (cf. Bartsch 1998). Under another perspective, for example of how the person feels or how he behaves socially, we might understand the metaphoric use of the word *snail* as creating a new concept that is a metaphor of the concept of sliminess or stickiness in the social sphere.

Even if we merely have similarity sets in contrast to each other, under a certain perspective, without associated terms, namely representatives of concepts that are not linguistically expressed, even then a perspective change can create the possibility to integrate or understand data that do not fit into the available conceptual system without names. A new perspective may single out a new similarity set among the old data, or it selects data from an old similarity set such that the new unusual datum fits together with this newly selected similarity set, and thus gets integrated into it, and hereby is understood. In this creative way of understanding, in which a change to a new perspective takes place, a new concept is formed, which is a new way of understanding data. Here we have a basic pre-form of metaphorical understanding of a situation or object without having a linguistic term to transfer. If we want to use a sign we then could use a picture, for example the picture of an eagle, by which we could order a man into a series of eagle experiences or stereotypical knowledge about eagles, under the perspective of strength and ranking in power. But also without any sign this pre-form of metaphorical understanding is possible. It is just the usual way of concept formation and understanding, except for the use of another perspective than that which has been used previously for registering similarity between a series of situations or individuals.

A parallel story about understanding a situation can be told with reference to the neurological processes involved: Causal effects of the situation (received data) activate those groups of neurons that function as conceptual indicators and individual concept indices with their connected concept indicators that have been established by confronting and experiencing earlier similar situations. Activation circuits are established that correspond to constituents of the situation. They are bound together in larger, synchronized circuits of activation, which correspond to larger constituents, and to the whole situation.

> (2)   *Understanding a linguistic utterance* first means that the utterance is understood as a linguistic episode. The linguistic understanding of a linguistic episode or utterance, as acoustic and phonetic, phonological, lexical and syntactic understanding of the utterance as an utterance of an expression (linguistic type, that is the linguistic concept in distinction from the situational or semantic concept) has a similar built-up as the situational understanding, that is the situational concept. By the linguistic understanding the utterance is conceptualized as a linguistic expression or utterance type.

Understanding the semantic value of an utterance, on the other hand, means understanding the expression within the utterance situation and the present context. Of course, the present situational and contextual restrictions on the semantic understanding can influence the assignment of a linguistic type to the utterance, because the conceptual semantics of the utterance type, the expression, has to be such that it fits into the context and situation.

Understanding here consists in construing satisfaction situations for the expression, and especially the sentence, by forming B-intersections, that is by forming Binding-intersections as constituents: In a Binding-intersection between two concepts the smallest situational concept is formed that is embeddable into both concepts under preservation of stability and/or coherence. This smallest situational concept is the type of all the satisfaction situations that satisfy not just both concepts separately ("intersection"), rather they satisfy both, the two concepts, and also the syntactic synthesis between them. For example, understanding the phrase *brown horse* does not only mean that the possible satisfaction situations for this expression have to fit into the concept BROWN and into the concept HORSE under preservation of stability. This would be the case already for a situation in which there is something brown, i.e. the situation fits (salva stabilitate) into a series of brown-examples, and in which something else is a horse, i.e. the situation fits (salva stabilitate) into a series of horse-examples. But this would not yet be a satisfaction situation for *brown horse*. Rather the expression moreover means that the satisfaction situation must be the smallest in which both conditions are fulfilled. This is an extra condition: according to the syntactic value of the construction, each satisfaction situation of the expression must contain a single object that fits into the concept BROWN as well as into the concept HORSE, under preservation of stability. *Understanding a phrase* in this way is

1. collecting the restrictions on possible satisfaction situations of the phrase by intersecting representations of the concepts involved (namely intersecting stabilizing sets of examples or satisfaction situations of the concepts involved), which is lexical understanding
2. forming, according to the syntactic analysis, syntactic understanding, the smallest situational concepts that characterize within these intersections the satisfaction situations for the constituents of the phrase and finally for the whole phrase or sentence. Construing a smallest situation is illustrated by the following example.

Understanding the sentence *John beats Paul*

The possible alternative hierarchies of syntactic construction all lead to the same result, a representative set, a representation, of the situational concept of John beating Paul. Such a set of situations in which John beats Paul can be represented by the smallest situation, or situation type, in which John beats Paul, here represented by E. It can be broken down into different constituent structures, all leading to the same result.

$$E = \mathbf{B}(\mathbf{B}(\mathbf{B}(John, Agent), Beat), \mathbf{B}(Paul, Patient))$$
$$E = \mathbf{B}(\mathbf{B}(\mathbf{B}(Paul, Patient), Beat), \mathbf{B}(John, Agent))$$
$$E = \mathbf{B}(\mathbf{B}(Beat, \mathbf{B}(John, Agent)), \mathbf{B}(Paul, Patient))$$
$$E = \mathbf{B}(\mathbf{B}(Beat, \mathbf{B}(Paul, Patient)), \mathbf{B}(John, Agent))$$
$$E = \mathbf{B}(\mathbf{B}(\mathbf{B}(John, Agent), \mathbf{B}(Paul, Patient)), Beat)$$
$$E = \mathbf{B}(\mathbf{B}(\mathbf{B}(Paul, Patient), \mathbf{B}(John, Agent)), Beat)$$

We see that the process of construing the complex situational concept E consists in gathering constraints on the set of possible satisfaction situations for the sentence at issue; in understanding the sentence step by step, more and more constraints are placed on the set of possible satisfaction situations, by which the set becomes smaller. The process of understanding a sentence thus is a specification, which can be done in different orders, but which always involves certain fixed hierarchies, namely the combination of the role-concepts with the participant individual concepts, and the binding of these with the action or event concept. Otherwise, the conceptual semantic structure is flat, and can be broken down into different constituent structures, depending on pragmatic factors. We can, for example, take John as topic and Beat Paul as focus, as in *John beats Paul* uttered with normal intonation, or we can take Paul as topic and John Beats as focus as in *JOHN beats Paul*, or in *Paul is beaten by John* uttered with normal intonation.

We have merely treated the conceptual understanding. Interpreting an utterance presupposes conceptual understanding, but it also needs interpreting determiners, anaphoric pronouns and deictic expressions, especially temporal and local deixis, which will not be treated here. – On these topics there exists an extensive literature in Formal Semantics. – It would require taking into account self-reference and awareness of ones own position in space and time, in order to fix the deixis to places, times, objects, and situations from out the point of view of the speaker or observer. In this relationship we establish indices for situations and individuals, which is beyond the present topic, and it also would make use of indices, a procedure that will be introduced more explicitly in the chapter on memory.

3.   There is a relationship between understanding a situation and understanding an utterance. We construe satisfaction-situations from uttered sentences, and we construe sentences by understanding a situation and then describing it according to this conceptualization.

4.   There is a parallel between **B**-intersections, binding between concepts according to constituent structures, and the embedding of smaller activation circuits into larger ones, on the neural side. The structure of activation circuits embedded into larger circuits emerges in consciousness as the structure of smaller constituents embedded into larger constituents (confer for the argumentation for this assumption to Bartsch 2002: Chap. 2 and 3).

There is a further kind of understanding, namely understanding the other as performing speech acts and reporting propositional attitudes, and understanding the other by empathy, especially through trying to see something from the other's point of view. Inter-subjective and subjective aspects in conceptualization play a role in how far this understanding of the other goes. I shall not treat this topic here, but it is partly taken into account in Bartsch (1998), in the chapter on propositional attitudes.

5.   How memory works in understanding

We have just answered this question of how memory works in understanding for the general memory, and especially for the semantic memory.

Also the historical, specific memory plays a role in understanding, of course as far as reference to individuals is concerned, which has been shown in the previous example, but also the episodic memory plays a role.

Above, it has been pointed out that the historical memory consists of groups of neurons that serve as indices for individuals, places, and episodes. The memory-indices have to be connected to the general concept indicators that had characterized aspects of the previously experienced individual or episode. They have also to be connected to indicators of temporal and local relationships relating them to each other and to indices for the perceiver's local and temporal position, in order to establish deictic reference. Likewise, the indices are connected to category indicators of the sensorial systems (indicators of sensorial concepts) and to neurons on the primary sensorial fields, which are dedicated to effecting certain sensations, certain smells, sounds, faces, feelings of movements and other proprioceptional sensations, and emotions. A certain aspect, which is identical to one in the current situation, can via suitable connections call up a remembrance of a previous situation containing that aspect. Hereby the remembered episode is constructed via the connections from the memory indices to conceptual indicators and neurons of the other fields. This will be elaborated further in Chapter 2.

In understanding, the current situation is "seen in the light of" one or more previous similar situations: aspects from these situations can be mixed up or partly be replaced for each other; and the current situation can be experienced with additional aspects from the old situations. The two situations or episodes can also be consciously compared or contrasted. Singular actions, but also routines that were connected with an old situation can be re-activated to become part of the current situation; they can be imagined, planned, or executed.

The indices that, by their connections to conceptual indicators, constitute the structure of the remembered episode are connected to each other in activation. Furthermore, the indices can be connected to other episodes, which can be called up by activation of these connections. If, for example, we experience often that Peter beats other boys, some of these previously experienced episodes of Peter beating others can be called up, since the connections are already strengthened by these repeated experiences. This also means that these episodes are typical within the individual concept we have of Peter. An individual concept thus gets indicated by an index that is connected with indicators of typical properties of the individual, and that is connected with indices of episodes in which we have experienced the individual or about which we have been told.

Both, the general memory of concepts and routines, especially the semantic memory, and the specific, historical memory, especially the individuating and the episodic memory, make up our understanding and even our perception of new situations and new sentences. Understanding is subjective, and for a great part inter-subjectively coordinated at the same time, through the workings of the partially common historical memory of a community of people and the partially common general memory, especially its linguistically guided semantic part. This inter-subjective part is, of course, the essential part for being able to get informed about the surroundings not merely by one's own experience, but by experience that is coordinated with others and by getting informed through others about all that one does not, or even cannot, experience oneself, though it still is relevant for one's own orientation and possibility to act. Concept formation is steered by the objective surroundings, in which the learning and experiencing individual lives, and about which it has to be informed and has to act; concept formation is subjective in part, depending on personal experiences; but concept formation is also inter-subjectively guided by the conventions and norms of the communities, especially the language communities, in which the subject lives. In this way we are able to share our experiences in as far as they can be informative to others.

In the following chapters, the model of the memory as a capacity of remembering will be elaborated further, then be related to Bergson's exposition on memory and matter, and finally will be used as a means for interpreting Marcel Proust's novel *A la Recherche du temps perdu* (English translation: *Remembrance of Things Past*) as a concrete exposition of our capacity of concept formation and understanding.

CHAPTER 2

Memory

Memory is divided at least into two kinds, mostly called semantic memory and fact-memory, or semantic memory and episodic memory. Since not all general concepts, including relationships, are linguistically, and especially lexically expressed, we more precisely could speak of the generalizing memory, or short "general memory", and a part of it, which is the semantic memory, being directly associated with lexical items expressing general concepts. We will also take the procedural memory to be part of the general memory, since procedures or routines are generalizations, now not of observed events, but of own actions and activities. Besides the episodic memory we distinguish another individualizing memory, the individual concepts memory, which holds our concepts of individuals, including individual objects. The episodic memory and the individual concept memory together are referred to as the specific (historical) memory, distinct from the generalizing memory. Sometimes, the episodic memory is also called the autobiographic memory. For an overview of kinds and function of the memory confer to, for example, Haberlandt (1999).

Conway (2001a, b) makes a distinction between episodic memory and autobiographic memory. Next to the working memory (or short term memory) that covers a time span of seconds to a minute or so, the episodic memory covers up to 24 hours. The episodes from the episodic memory get organized and hereby consolidated in the autobiographic memory that extends over a life span. The organization, according to Conway, happens by relating the episodes to a structure of goals that determines what the self is. In the autobiographic memory congruence is achieved by modifications of episodes, or beliefs, or goals, such that they fit to each other. I think that the notion of one autobiographic memory organized by the self as a structure of goals is much to narrow. A person is not a self by being held together by a goal structure. It is more the body and our bodily feelings in relation to and as part of our surroundings that make us experience episodes as something that involves our self. Furthermore, being goal-directed in an organized way is very much imposed on an individual by a certain culture and a particular social background. It is also an old idea that humans overall are rational, that is goal-directed and tend to behave adequate to the goals they have. But that is not quite true, and certainly not all that determines a person's life. Accordingly, we do not have merely one single biography, but several ones, namely partial concepts of ourselves depending on certain perspectives we take. In the context of applying for a professional position we will present quite a different curriculum vitae than in the context of a social intercourse with a friend, or with one's husband, or one's wife. Here, goals will not figure prominently in the order between episodes of ones life that are selected. There are very different orderings among the episodes of ones life-history, depending on contexts in which one represents one's own self to others and to oneself in self-reflection, and the question is how far one can succeed in making these different selves consistent with each other to form a coherent whole.

It is not necessary to assume a distinction between episodic and autobiographical memory because it is merely a matter of consolidation whether an episode will be remembered for a longer time. This consolidation can take place by rehearsing the episode consciously or also, part of it, merely unconsciously after it had been experienced, possibly also in a good nights sleep.

Our memory is built up in learning processes and generally in experiencing situations, and also in understanding narratives. In a way, every experience is part of a learning process. It attributes to building up and to modifying general concepts, and it can give rise to a more or less lasting specific remembrance, in which an experienced situation or object is connected with emotional and motivational aspects and motor dispositions towards behavior and especially actions. Such aspects later on, when experienced again, can call up a previous situation in which they prominently figured, and thus can give rise to remember related episodes, individuals, and places. In this way we are able to "regain time again", as Proust formulates it in his great novel, which will be the source for illustrations of the properties of memory in the following essay on memory, understanding, and consciousness. The structural properties of memory treated here are derived from the requirements a dynamic conceptual and referential semantics imposes on what our memory must be like.

Remembering is a conscious state, but even if a remembrance of a previous episode similar to the current one is not achieved in consciousness, the perception and understanding of the current situation can be modified or partly determined by the unconscious partial reconstruction process of the previous situation, and actions can be called up by the current situation via the unconscious links to the previous episode. Thus an action, or attitude, or emotional evaluation will be transplanted on, or associated with the current situation, though we are not aware of where they come from.

1.   The architecture of memory

In Figure 1 below, the proposed architecture of the working episodic memory is represented. All two-way directed arrows represent circuits consisting of a connection with one direction and a connection with a reciprocal direction. In the central field **M** of the episodic memory, an episode is registered by a group of indices. The indices are established in the process of understanding the original episode by selecting those neurons as indices that are strongest activated in **M** by activation traveling via connections from the sensorial and motor fields and the conceptual and routine maps and the emotional and evaluation maps and the proprioception maps, and possibly get furthermore activated from out neurons in the pre-frontal cortex, which might serve as indices in the working or short-term memory, which are built up in perceiving or imagining an episode (see further Sections 2 and 3 of this chapter). In the constituent circuits of activation established in understanding by the activity traveling along the forward connections and their reciprocal ones, the strongest connections will later on be the paths along which most likely the episode is re-called. The selected neurons are established as more or less stable indices for the respective, hereby memorized, episode by strengthening the connections between these neurons and the neurons activated at the same time in the other maps or fields in the repeated circuit activation in re-experiencing, re-understanding and emotionally re-acting to the episode, as well as in subsequent imagining the episode in remembrance.

Considering the basic semantic structures of episodes, we can expect that the indices would work best in a process of binding general concepts together in ontologically relevant aspects, if the indices were to point or connect to indices of individual concepts, and to the indicators of relationships of space-time order, and of general concepts and relations. And they have to connect to (currently employed) neurons on the sensorial fields, which hereby will be used in forming and imagining the remembered episode. If the currently experienced situation and the remembered situation are both distinctly conscious in perception and imagination, this must happen in alternation, will they not be mixed up, and in this alternation they can be compared and even contrasted with respect to the details. But we can also expect that the current situation and the previous situation get blended together within the currently perceived situation, and thus we see the current situation more or less in the light of the previously experienced situation, even when that situation is not, or cannot, be remembered distinctly. The memory indices of the previous episode get activated by the indicators involved in the activation circuits of the current episode on other fields, and also re-activate them. Thus a rhythmic, synchronized state of activation of interconnected circuits can build up, which, when hitting the sensorial, motor, emotional and proprioceptional fields, brings about the consciously perceived current episode, which can be a merger of the old and the new, or which can alternate with the remembrance of the old episode.

The following Figure 1 presents a rough architecture of how the center of the specific memory (**IC** and **M**) interacts in circuit activation with other cognitively relevant neuronal fields. The boxes in this figure show the two central parts of the specific, historical, memory treated here, namely the individual concept memory and the episodic memory. The two-way directed arrows from and to indicators and indices in the respective maps or fields stand for activation circuits that together can form compositions, being in a certain rhythm or resonance due to the firing of the neurons involved. In a remembrance of an episode the activation circuits form a whole of smaller and larger circuits that also include activation circuits with groups of neurons on the sensorial, motor, emotional, and proprioceptual fields. Including these neurons, which are dedicated to phenomenal expression, provides the phenomenal material ('qualia'), integrated into the conceptual structure of the episode. This is necessary for a conceptually structured episode emerging in consciousness. Argumentation for this claim can be found in Bartsch (2002).

The specific memory field, which contains episodic and individual indices, is closely connected with emotional, proprioceptual, sensorial fields, with fields of indicators for general concepts and with routine and motor fields. From all these fields, memories of episodes can be induced. In principle, memories are constructed by connectivity, based on similarity and association selected under perspectives, which are created by contexts of actions, desires, emotions, and active beliefs. Memory is a constructive ability, not a store or collection of propositions or images. Also the remembrance of an sentence utterance or inscription is an episode, namely a linguistic episode.

Both kinds of memory, the general memory and the specific memory, have connections with the sensorial, motor, emotional, evaluative, and proprioceptional areas. By interaction circuits between indicators in these areas and indices in the historical memory we perceive and imagine episodes (linguistic as well as situational ones).

In the Cognitive Science literature, the close connection between the hippocampus and the amygdala, the emotion-field, has been investigated, among others, in psychological and neurological research about the role of strong emotions, affections, and arousal in consolidating memories of episodes, especially as those that get a place in the narratives of the autobiographic memory.

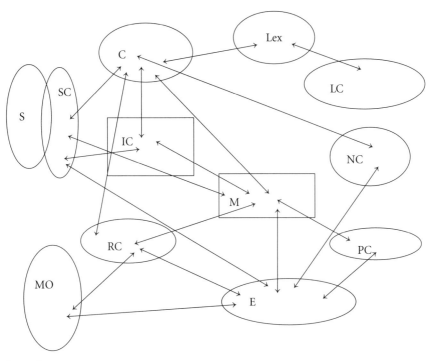

Legenda:
M   episodic memory base
MO   (pre)-motor fields
RC   routine maps (concepts/categories of routines)
E   emotional fields and emotional concepts/categories maps
PC   proprioceptual fields
NC   maps for normative and evaluative concepts/rules
LC   linguistic concepts: syntactic categories, syntactic patterns/rules
Lex   lexical maps
C   general concepts/ontological categories maps
IC   individual concepts memory base
S   sensorial fields
SC   sensorial concepts/categories, including face map

Figure 1.

The role of affect with respect to the accuracy of memories of certain episodes is the main topic of the articles edited by Winograd and Neisser (1992), which report on research about the so-called "flashbulb" memories of unexpected and emotional events. It has been found that the recollections elicited shortly after and some years after the event are often inconsistent, which puts the accuracy into question. In accordance with Wagenaar (1986), it has been found that later elicitations are more consistent with the early ones if the memorizing had been supported, in the first place, by writing down the events in a diary in a fashion organized by cueing questions such as *what, where, when, how, why, who took part?* These questions constitute the constituent structure of a situation and of its descriptions. What the affection contributes to accuracy depends on the contents of the memories and on the kind of affection. Self-affection had a stronger effect than empathy with others, who where involved in the original event. The developmental studies report that young children, who see less or no causal links between an episode and other episodes or surrounding situations, remember less accurately. Probably due to less embedding of the episode into the contiguity with other situations, they are less able to distinguish what they have experienced themselves from what they have heard or have seen pictures of. The articles generally support the model of the constructive memory and the idea that there is no special memory devise for "flashbulb" memories.

The linguistic concept maps (LC), containing indicators for morpho-syntactic categorization, and the lexical maps (**Lex**) are connected in activation circuits with certain sensorial concepts maps for speech perception and with routine maps for articulation. The overall architecture that functions in recognizing and producing linguistic forms has not been represented in Figure 1. In principle, it is just a part of our overall memory, containing indicators for linguistic patterns on different linguistic levels (phonetic, phonological, morphological, lexical) and syntactic categories and indices for construing sentence constituents and whole sentences. Also the built-up of a linguistic phrase works along reciprocal connections between indicators and indices, and it is realized in articulatory, auditive, or visual phenomenal material by circuit activation with these areas.

The lexical maps (**Lex**), possibly for several languages, have per indicator for a lexical item, and also for repeatedly used phrases, associative relationships via connections to other indicators of linguistic items forming its regular linguistic distribution, and also to the indicators of linguistic categories and sub-categories in LC that characterize the linguistic distribution. Likewise, in parallel, the general concept maps have per concept indicator associative relationships via connections to other concept indicators for concepts that characterize the surrounding of the concept-realization in a situation. These indicators for associative relationships characterize contiguity relationships within and between situations. The regularly surrounding concepts functioning in these relationships are indicated by general ontological concept indicators such that in this way the conceptual frame of a concept and the corresponding syntactic-semantic frame of the concept-representing lexical item is represented in this structure of relationships between indicators. The frames give the basic conceptually motivated syntactic-semantic order in linguistic representations, which are expressed by conventional linguistic patterning and rules. Syntactic categories are similarity sets based on similarity by semantic and syntagmatic relationships, namely by analogies, whereby syntagmatic relationships are the contiguity relationships in phrases and sentences.

The individual concept base (**IC**) consists of indices for individuals. These indices, when activated, point via connections to (1) indicators of properties (grasped by us as the general concepts we construct as ordering structures on growing sets of data) and indicators of relationships in connection with indices for other individuals, and (2) indices of episodes in which the individual is known to have been involved in as a participant. The central field of the episodic memory (**M**), the episodic memory base, and the IC-field of indices for individual concepts together form a compound map of indices, to be called the *specific memory base* (**SPM**), which consists of a field with indices for individual concepts, and a field of indices for episodes and, possibly, relations between them. This specific memory corresponds to having two kinds of basic entities in our ontology, namely individuals and situations/events.

We distinguish indicators and indices, the *indicators* being assemblies of neurons that are activated in perceiving instances or creating instances for a concept or relationship in performance. Thus motor routines, which form the so-called procedural memory, are a kind of general concepts and are here taken to be part of the general memory, which thus comprises the procedural memory. In circuit activation with sensorial and motor fields such an assembly of neurons functions as a conceptual (or routine) indicator. The indicators with their connections to other indicators and to the sensorial, proprioceptional, emotional, and (pre-) motor areas form the generalizing memory, and especially a subsection of it, the semantic memory, in as far as the indicators are associated to linguistic expressions denoting the corresponding concepts.

The *indices* on the other hand are assemblies of neurons in the specific memory, those that refer to episodes, situations, events, and to individuals. An index for an individual, together with its connections to the indicators of concepts and relationships that are known to characterize and identify the individual, functions as an individual concept. Since not all episodes and objects which we encounter are remembered, we assume that there are many indices which loose their connections to the activated indicators of the index-establishing episode or object fast and are thus only binding together the respective concepts into the unity of the experienced episode or object for a short time. These memory indices then form the basis for a short-term memory, lasting for seconds or up to 5 to 10 minutes in understanding a sentence utterance or a situation (see also Section 3 of this chapter about the working memory and the possible location of these indices), and in dealing with it in text-interpretation or in argumentation. These neurons might be re-usable for functioning as different indices. When they have lost their connections they might again be available for organizing and shortly remembering new episodes. In this way they still contribute to establishing the generalizing and associating memory, this means to our concepts and routines, by binding these together into situations and situational concepts (types) of repeated situations.

From research reporting about the chemistry and physiology of the brain, which has been performed by neuro-scientists, we know that it is a matter of the availability of certain chemicals, proteins and enzymes, that make connections function in the transmission of electric charge over the synapses, and that make the synapses grow broader and thicker, such that the connections get strong and serve for a long time for transmitting charges by means of neurotransmitters. The production and availability of the required chemicals varies for different brain areas and changes with the state of health and the states of being awake or asleep. Forgetting is due to loss of neurons and/or loss of connections between neurons, such that these cannot function as indices or indicators.

Consolidation of indices, and herewith of memories, means that their connections with the other indices and indicators that were involved in perceiving and understanding the episode get strengthened by rehearsal. Loss of the connections means that the indices cease to be indices and are then just neurons that may be available for fixing new memories. Generally speaking, indices and indicators are indices and indicators merely in virtue of their connections to other indices and indicators, and finally to sensorial, motor, proprioceptual, and emotional indicators, and their causal connectedness to our natural and social surroundings. Without these connections they are just neurons without employment.

The indices must get ordered at least partly by spatial and temporal relationships, which primarily must have been established by forming indicators for relationships of temporal and spatial order when experiencing basic bodily movements. (How a relational indicator works in circuit activation is presented in Section 2 of this chapter.) In self-experience, for example, positions of the hands, or the movements of the tongue in the mouth, can be felt (through activation in the proprioception areas) as taking time, following each other, and as filling space, moving through space, and hereby creating the experience of distances. Starting from feeling space and time in sequences and relative locations of bodily activity, the relationships get enriched by finding such relationships also in outer space around the body, and then generally finding these relationships among objects and episodes in the outer world, which also get ordered in space and time. We have to assume such a development of temporal and spatial concepts because without a basis in our feeling of bodily activity we never could experience and thus be conscious of space-time order.

We have assumed that the sensorial, proprioceptional, emotional, and (pre-) motor areas in our brain contain the neurons that are dedicated to produce feelings that are the phenomenal basis for being aware of something in a conscious manner. The indicators and indices themselves, together with their connections, merely form a system of pointers that function via activation going along the established connections. We might sometimes indirectly be aware of brain activity in thinking, for example, when we try hard to remember a certain word, phrase or name, but for some time do not quite succeed, and try all kind of associations via situational contexts and via linguistic contexts to get at the name we can not remember at the moment. We feel that we are close to it, but not quite get it. We get results that do not survive control, which means that when we perceive these results they get "played back" in the process of understanding and are experienced as not fitting to the intentions or our images of the object for which we want to find the right word. If we are lucky, some of the contexts will pick up the word. From the structure of activation circuits due to imagining or perceiving this context there then happened to be a functioning connection to the indicator of the word we were searching for. Thus, search is not a method of defining a cue and a criterion of verification and processing through large storages of files in order to find something matching the cue and then verifying in a control unit what has been found.

The bureaucratic model of search, as it is implemented in computers, is not an adequate picture of how search in memory goes on. Conway and Pleydell-Pearce (2000) have modified this classic model somewhat, but still they clinch to it. They still write in terms of "retrieval", "representations", "elaboration of a cue", "setting of a verification criterion in a retrieval model", which sounds very much like a bureaucratic search model for something which is not a rationally guided process but just naturally comes or does not come to us by activation of connections from whatever source that happened to be connected to some aspect of what is searched for. And it is well-known that whether a connection can function or not depends on many physiological and anatomic factors, some of which can be influenced by stimulations from the outside. Conway and Pleydell-Pearce (2000) also refer to rising activations in certain brain areas, and they write: "a specific autobiographical memory is a pattern of activation across the indices of the autobiographical knowledge base conjoined with a sub-set of activated working-self goals" (2000: 273). They try to relate the neurological description to their psychological model of memory, but still mix up the terminology of traditional cognitive psychology with neurological terminology, like in the sentence quoted above, where an activation pattern (neurological) is conjoined with goals (psychological). Conway's model still is inspired by the metaphor of the computer, whereby the hardware stands for the brain and the software for the psychological model of the hidden mind. All human activities are reconstructed as due to rational processes in a hidden mind. However, the terminology inspired by the functioning of the computer is not adequate to the functioning of the human brain. We humans are able to rational processes, but these must take place on the level of conscious phenomena and objects and situations in the world. There we have representations, which we can dissect, decompose, re-compose, transform, replace, put in logical order, or move around according to overt rules, habits, or just for fun. On this level we also can handle criteria, verification, justified evaluation, and control. All this we can do in our mind, which is conscious and open. There is no hidden mind, but just the brain and body.

We cannot feel what is going on in our head in detail, or what processes of thinking are going on, except when the interaction circuits hit the areas that provide for the qualitative aspects, the qualia, of phenomenal effects. The whole system of pointers would not mean anything if it were not for the inclusion of the areas in the brain dedicated to phenomenal quality, namely the sensorial, motor, proprioceptional, and emotional fields. They make the connection to the world of bodies, objects, and episodes by being primarily affected by this world in certain ways, and by having effects on this world. These resulting affections and also the effects get ordered in repetition and re-activating practices, by circuit activation between these phenomenally dedicated areas and the general and the specific memory, i.e. the systems of indicators, indices, and their connections. These circuit processes give rise to structured objects and episodes, being the phenomenal results of the interaction circuits in a state of rhythmic, synchronized activation between the phenomenally active areas, i.e. the conceptual, sensorial, motor, emotional, and proprioceptional areas, and the memory areas; and by connecting to linguistically specialized areas, they give rise to the appropriate linguistic representations, and in turn can be re-activated via the input of linguistic utterances.

The indices must be underlying our acts of reference, since they organize also the structure in which reference to situations takes place, namely ordered in constituents. We thus can take them as pointers to what we refer to in real or imagined situations. Since we use them in understanding, perceiving and imagining, as well as in remembering, indices must be used in the processes of short term and of long-term memory.

There is a vast and daily growing neuro-scientific literature, which reports about detailed research on observed activation of neural areas and even single cells, in connection with performed isolated cognitive tasks. Though it is important to see whether these findings are compatible with a semantically motivated model of neural architecture, as it is explored in the present essay, they are on the one hand too detailed (concerning physiological processes) and on the other hand to global (concerning activation in certain areas) to essentially contribute to the formulation of the structural requirements on the architecture of brain processes that can serve to perform the functions of a dynamic conceptual and referential syntax and semantics. Therefore in the present essay, this literature is not taken into account in a systematic way, though incidentally some of this research is mentioned, whenever it provides some interesting details concerning the working of the memory, although it deals on a much more fine-grained level of description.

The model of the constructive memory, as it is developed here under the perspective of dynamic conceptual semantics, is supported by the ecological/cognitive position on the construction of the Self through the episodic memory, documented by the articles collected by Neisser and Fivush (Eds., 1994). These articles report a great flexibility of remembering. What is reported as remembered depends on the context of the situation in which the remembrance occurs. Strong emotions connected with the episode are selective of what will be remembered, as are the contiguity or context of local and temporal and of causal and motivational connectedness in which the episode is embedded. Such contexts help to remember correctly. Each act of recalling a memory, as also other experiences previous to the recall change it, because it enhances a selection of aspects from the previous episode that is remembered, and it might add other aspects, induced by the present situation of remembrance. So-called remembrances can be true, partly false, and even totally false fabrications, due to suggestions made by analysts or other communication partners. Strong emotions can strengthen remembrance, but in other cases can also repress remembrance, or lead to false remembrances, such as in several cases of so-called child abuse that turned out to be false, or at least inaccurate. Accuracy cannot expected to be perfect, but there must be some truth to most remembrances, because without it the utility of memory would be zero and it would not have been developed in evolution. Generally it can be stated that accuracy

LIBRARY OF DAVIDSON COLLEGE

decreases if a person wants to uphold and support a certain personal attribute essential for his propagated self-image. Accuracy increases when there are more cues for the remembrance (Winograd, p. 243).

Several authors in Neisser and Fivush (1994) argue that the Self is a narrative construction in which autobiographic episodes are embedded into "cultural models of self-construction" (Barclay, p. 56), often strikingly generic as self-accounts influenced and organized by patterns and idealized roles common in our culture (Bruner, p. 51). The Self is primarily a product of thought, using specific remembrances and other general cognitive capacities in construing a consistent course of life, sometimes governed by a certain point of view, such as being an agent, or being a victim (Bruner, p. 43). On the other hand, especially with respect to amnesia patients, it is pointed out that they cannot have such a constructed autobiographic self; rather they still have a perceived self and an interpersonal self, provided by the people they live with (Neisser, p. 15, 16). Autobiographic remembering is seen largely as an improvisational act, creating "proto-selves", depending on expectations with respect to the audience and on knowledge of cultural genres of representation. It requires attention and feedback from others (Barclay, p. 71). Also individuals often invoke implicit theories to construct their past, mostly concerning certain desirable personal attributes, showing in traits, feelings, and behavior (Ross & Buehler, p. 208). By such a governing implicit theory they create coherence and stability of their autobiographic Self. In opposition to the authors who stress coherence and stability of the autobiographic self, some authors point out that there is not one self constructed by an individual. Rather many selves are improvised (Barclay, Albright). The multiplicity of selves one remembers depends on the present situation, the audience, and on past experiences. Making selves happens by "skillful improvisations" rather than by direct retrieval. The autobiographic self, as it appears in different settings of self-presentation, is a construction, which is always partial, but it is "assuming coherence over vast stretches of oblivion"; these numerous such selves of one biological person partly consist of images, partly they are verbally expressed (Albright, p. 30 and 33). Remembering is a skill that is first learned by young children in social settings (Neisser, p. 11), formed by "parental memory styles" (Fivush, p. 137), which are the different ways of parents talking with their children of past events.

2.   Remembering, structured from out the episodic memory base

In our brain, the area we have called **M** is essential for having an episodic memory, i.e. for remembering past episodes, which we have encountered in our
surroundings, or about which we have had linguistically coded information.

What this area really does is not quite clear. Neurologists have found out
that if this area, the hippocampus, is damaged in patients, they cannot remember episodes they have experienced in the past, and/or they cannot remember
episodes they have experienced after the damage, depending on where exactly
the lesion is, and on how extensive it is.

It is, by now, a passed-by stage to think of memory as a kind of huge library
in which propositions and pictures are stored about previous experiences, and
from where somehow such propositions and pictures can be drawn out into
the open, i.e. into consciousness, when the memory is triggered in appropriate ways. This century-old picture for the storage of empirical knowledge in
our minds we find already in Plato's dialogue Theaitetos, where he uses the
metaphors of the waxen tablet and the pigeon house. In remembering we find
an inscription on the waxen tablet, or we catch a pigeon from the many we
have put into the house, each pigeon representing a stored episode or fact.
Plato rejects these metaphors as inappropriate for how knowledge (episteme)
is available to us, though he thinks they are partly correct for episodic knowledge (doxa). If this picture of storage is incorrect, as we now know, how then
can we think about what memory is and how it functions?

It has been observed that remembering is more a reconstruction of an
episode, in which the same sensory areas in the brain are involved as have
been involved when experiencing the original episode. Experiments (Kreiman,
Koch, & Fried 2000) have shown that persons who have seen a certain picture,
for example Mona Lisa, have for about 90% the same brain areas activated in
the act of recollecting the picture, as they had when they previously perceived
the picture. The small difference is easily explained, because in perceiving they
had a slightly different, mainly more detailed, and circumstantial input to the
brain's visual system than they had in the act of recollection; and in recollection
aspects might have been added that had not originally been in the picture.

What then is the task of area **M**? We can think of it as a collection of indices, whereby a neuron or a small group of neurons serves as an index, or
as a combination of indices. An index gets established as a group of neurons
that is activated when the sensorial-cognitive-emotional-and motor, and proprioception systems form the perception and the whole personal uptake of
an episode, which hereby is a perceived and therewith located, conceptualized

(apectualized), and emotionally evaluated episode, short: it is an understood episode. The activated parts of the brain, i.e. the activated conceptual indicators on the generalizing conceptual maps of ontological categories and of habits or routines, the individual concept indices with their connections to indicators of general concepts characterizing the individual, the neurons of the primary sensorial fields, the groups of neurons serving as conceptual indicators for basic forms, motions, colors, and faces on the maps of the visual system, and the conceptual indicators of other sensory modalities involved, as well as proprioception areas of motion and emotion, all take part in forming the experienced episode. All these get directly or indirectly connected by synaptic activity and accordingly synaptic growth, whereby connections are established and strengthened to one or more neurons in area M, which then function as episodic indices, possibly also activating each other (pointing to each other) and indicators for temporal and local ordering relationships, and activating back the indicators on the other areas from which they had been activated.

The activation happens along circuits: in assembly X of neurons: excited neuron (1) → outgoing activation of (1) → incoming activation for neuron (2) → excitement of neuron (2) in assembly Y → outgoing activation of (2) → incoming activation for (1) → re-excitement of neuron (1) or some others of assembly X. Furthermore, neuron (2) can activate additional neurons along existing connections, which then can take part in the circuit activation if they are strongly enough activated (possibly also by other paths) and have reciprocal connections with neuron (2). Thus we might get the larger circuit (1) → (2) → (3) → (2) → (1), whereby also (1) → (3) → (1) can be induced. In the larger circuit, the smaller circuits (1) → (2) → (1) and (2) → (3) → (2) are embedded as constituents.

There have to be such circuits in order to strengthen and built up connections such that neurons in X can be activated from out area Y. If Y = M, the episodic memory center, this means that what goes into M from out some origin X, must also be able to go out from M back to the original X. In this way an index in M can point to conceptual indicators that had been activated in the original perception of a situation or object to which the establishment of the index in M is due, and thus can address the original contents that are remembered by inducing activation circuits between the respective conceptual indicators and the sensorial, motor, emotional and proprioceptional areas.

Note that we find no concepts on conceptual maps. We merely find groups of neurons that get activated with input of data from situations or objects of a certain kind. They are merely indicators of classification on the basis of similarities of incoming data with previous data. This amounts to the activa-

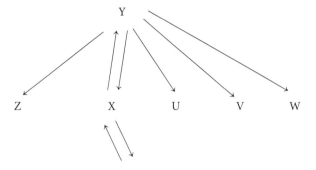

Figure 2.

tion traveling along connections strengthened by previous similar input, and they have associative connections with indicators for other concepts which had been formed and stabilized by experiencing other situations or objects that regularly stand in contiguity relationships of various kinds with the first situations and objects. We can say that the groups of neurons are conceptual indicators, pointers, and as such have a referential and categorizing semantic value, firstly by virtue of their connectedness with groups of neurons of the sensorial, motor, and emotional fields, activated by getting input from, and enacting on, the surroundings. Secondly, they have a structural semantic value by their connectedness to other conceptual indicators, following generalization or specification and following associations based on spatial, temporal, causal and other contiguity relationships.

The activation circuits for classificatory hierarchies and the ones for contiguity associations are typically of the following form:

(1) Classificatory hierarchy: X includes Y, for example "a rose is a flower":
     Y = FLOWER; X = ROSE.

In seeing or imagining a rose, the conceptual indicator for roses gets activated. The activation is spread further along an outgoing and incoming path to the indicator for flowers, which gets activated. It sends activation further to all the conceptual indicators for subsumed flower-concepts that had been learned. Since in this example only the ROSE-indicator is independently activated, only there the activation is strong enough to get an activation circuit going. The other indicators of different kinds of flowers get merely the fairly weak and broadly spread activation from the indicator of the hypernym, i.e. of the general flower-concept, and some more specific feature indicators by which certain flowers are similar to roses, and therefore activation circuits are not likely to be

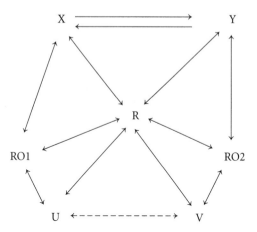

Figure 3.

formed there. Here the activation simply dies out without establishing circuits, if no additional activation comes about by some perspective change, for example by turning the attention to the question of what other flowers are prone to similar kinds of mildew disease.

(2)   Contiguity association: X has relationship R to Y

In order to avoid a drawing that gets too crowded by to many arrows, also here the doubly oriented arrow stands for an activation circuit. For a two-place relationship there must be two role-concept indicators which function to specify in which role X and in which role Y takes part in the relationship R. For example, if R is the causal relationship, ROLE 1 is Cause and ROLE 2 is Effect. The conceptual indicators involved are thus the ones for X, Y, R, RO1 and RO2. X and Y are activated in their causal relationship. Also for U and V the same relationship can be activated at the same time, if U and V receive independent activation. The activation circuits for U and V would make use of the same indicators R, RO1, and RO2, but should be in a different phase of neuron-spiking, in order to not be mixed up with those for X and Y.

That activation happens in circuits has been observed by neuro-scientists for the visual system and in the interconnection of the other brain areas and has a great explanatory power when assumed as an overall principle of brain architecture. The circuit structure generally provides a mode for representing constituent structure that can be found in experiencing situations, images, and linguistic expressions. This architecture implies that the indices can, when they receive some triggering activation from some brain part that had been involved in the experience of the original episode, send out activation along the previously established circuit-lines of sending back activity to those brain parts that had been the ones that originally have established the index in area **M** by activating the neuron or group of neurons that hereby had become indices. The indices in the area **M** must have been established with experiencing the original episode from out the neurons that express phenomenal quality, for example in the V1/V2 area of the visual system, where space-time contiguity ordering takes place in interaction with maps of form and motion, and self-perception, at least as far as one's own motor activity and directional orientation goes. In a parallel fashion, the respective maps of other sensorial modalities and proprioception can be involved. Likewise the indices in area **M** have to be associated via activated connections with the indicators of spatial and temporal concepts and of other concepts that had been activated by analyzing the original episode on the conceptual maps, that is, the fields containing conceptual indicators and their relationships.

The circuits go along the connections that had been activated in the understanding of the original episode, and possibly other similar episodes, and episodes connected with the original one by space-time and other factual contiguity. The whole activation in circuits has to include the primary sensorial areas, the proprioception and motor areas, areas of bodily feelings, and emotional areas, in order for us to experience an episode, as perceived or imagined or remembered. The circuit structure of smaller embedded circuits and larger composed circuits provides the possible constituent structures for episodes, as well as for the sentences describing these (cf. Bartsch 2002).

Empirical research and modeling of feedback loops between the prefrontal cortex and other cortical regions has been done and reported by Raffone and Wolters (2001). Supported by this research, we can assume that in order to keep the circuits between conceptual indicators in the generalizing and the sensorial and other areas going for a while, neurons in the prefrontal region connect with these indicators and seem to synchronize and enhance the spiking such that an oscillation of the involved circuitry is established as long as it is supported from these neurons activity. The prefrontal cortex thus maintains and segregates circuits of one episode from others by supporting one at a time, and as long as attention directed by some goal-directed activity keeps the supporting neurons active. In this way the prefrontal cortex supports the binding of conceptual indicators in circuits. There is thus maintenance of circuit activity and controlling by selective attention realized in the interaction with posterior cortex regions. On the other hand, change in attention and encoding activity desynchronizes circuits and gives room for building up new synchronized circuits. According to Raffone and Wolters (2001), the two functions of maintenance and control are characteristic for the working memory, which also contains the extra function of combinatorial coding. In our terms this means that the constituent built-up of circuit activation corresponding to our experience of situations and sentences is supported from out these functions of the working memory.

Logical combinations by truth-functional connectives and quantification, in our view, require representations of situations and sentences in consciousness, because these representations have to be evaluated for truth and falsity, such that correct combinations are secured. These (conscious) representations are taken to be conscious expressions of the circuits between neuronal assemblies in conceptual and sensor-motor areas, and they have to exist for a shorter or longer while in order to be combined and evaluated in the right way. Here the support by activated neurons of the prefrontal cortex seems important. As a means to keep up attention in the process of understanding a situation or a sentence, it also might be important for getting an episode encoded in episodic memory.

In the previous chapter we saw that in understanding a situation, individual concepts have to be made use of, by integrating the situation under a role-concept into a partial individual concept available under preservation of coherence of the individual concept. Thus, a situation was understood as the one of John beating Paul by integrating or embedding it into the partial individual concept of John as an actor and the partial individual concept of Paul as a patient and into the action concept of beating while binding them together into the smallest situation, and thus representing the situational concept that characterizes all situations in which John beats Paul. On the other hand, a sentence like *John beats Paul* was understood by forming the B-intersection, binding intersections, between the available partial individual concept of John and the role-concept AGENT, the B-intersection between the available individual concept of Paul with the PATIENT-concept, and then the B-intersections of these concepts of John as agent and Paul as patient with the action-concept of beating. This constituent structure of binding-intersections between concepts, now, corresponds to neuronal activation circuits along the connections between the groups of neurons serving as the respective concept indicators and indices. The smaller activation circuits are embedded into larger ones, and finally into the whole large circuit composed from all the constituent circuits. Now, also in remembering a past episode, a same kind of constituent structure is necessary in the remembrance; semantic-syntactic systematicity, the right organization of contiguity as far as this basic conceptual built up is concerned, must be preserved in the remembered episode, such that the situation of Peter

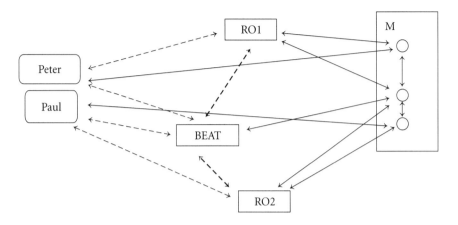

Figure 4. Memory activation of the episode "Peter beats Paul"

having beaten Paul is distinguished from the one of Paul having beaten Peter. This has to be steered from out the memory index, as we see in Figure 4.

The round-cornered rectangles represent the previously established individual concept indicators, consisting of their **IC**-indices and the concept indicators connected with these. The rectangles represent concept indicators.

In the example above, we have taken R (in Figure 3) as the Beat-action and RO1 as the Agent-role, and RO2 as the Patient-role. The rectangle on the right comprises the compound memory index of the episode. The dashed connections can be induced by the activated connections that were fixed in memory. The three memory indices depicted in the figure, of course, remind the reader schooled in formal semantics on the predicate-logical forms used since Davidson's article "The Logical Form of Action Sentences" (1967). In fact, the above figure of activation circuits can be mapped by an homomorphism on the logical form of action sentences, and it is isomorphic to the logical forms used in the semantics of situations by Bartsch (1995).

When we understand a sentence that refers to a situation experienced in the past, the memory index of the past situation is activated from out the description given in the sentence via the conceptual indicators addressed by the lexical items in the sentence and the syntactic structure. If we have no index of the situation established in the past, but get informed about it for the first time, such an index has to be created temporarily within the working memory and also the memory of reported facts, which is part of the specific memory. The index then has additional access to other aspects of the past situation and we hereby can remember more about the past situation than is expressed in the sentence. A narrative text can induce a series of memory indices, related to each other temporally, locally, and also by other contiguity relationships.

The memory index of the episode, a group of neurons, has to be composed out of sub-indices, smaller groups of neurons or singular neurons, which fix the respective constituents, such that the episode of Peter beating Paul is distinguished from the episode of Paul beating Peter. This requires that a sub-index connects strongly to the index of Peter and the indicator of the Agent-concept (RO1), another sub-index to the index of Paul and the indicator of the Patient-concept (RO2), and a third index to the indicator of the Beat-concept. Hereby the general connections of the Beat-indicator to the Agent-indicator and to the Patient-indicator makes the overall activation circuit possible, which combines the sub-circuits in one constituent structure. This then must include a circuit activation with the sensory-motor fields in order to result in a conscious remembrance.

The neurons that function as sub-indices for Peter and Paul, respectively, do this by being connected to indicators of concepts that typically characterize Peter and Paul, respectively (indicated by the rounded rectangles in Figure 4). An individual concept always is partially indicated by an index together with the indicators of concepts characterizing the individual in an act of recognition. An individual concept indicator thus is a network of reciprocal connections between an index for the individual and the indicators of the concepts characterizing it, and also with the indices for the specific episodes in which the individual was involved, as far as they are indexed in memory. From out the memory indices the circuit activation between the conceptual indicators gets induced. These induced activations circuits are represented by the dashed circuits). The circuits with the sensory-motor areas are not represented in the figure.

The same kind of processes must take place in achieving activation circuits for other constituents, corresponding to modifier-noun and modifier-verb constructions, adnominal and adverbial constructions. In remembering a situation in which there was a brown horse and a black blanket, the memory index for the situation must contain at least two sub-indices, which organize the binding of Brown to Horse and Black to Blanket respectively, in order to distinguish this situation from one in which there is a black horse and a brown blanket. If the black blanket was on the brown horse, there additionally has to be a sub-index connecting to the indicator of the two-place relationship "On". The sub-index connecting to the indicator of Horse must also have a connection to the indicator of the Bottom-role-concept, relating to the indicator of the concept On, and the sub-index connecting to the Blanket indicator must

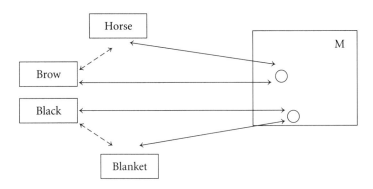

Figure 5. Memory activation of the episode "A brown horse and a black blanket"

also connect to the indicator of the Top-role, relating to the indicator of the concept On. Figure 5 merely shows two sub-indices of the memory index of a situation in which there is a brown horse and a black blanket. The two sub-indices organize the two constituents, such that Brown, Horse, Black, Blanket are not mixed up. The circuits organized from out the two indices in M should be in a different phase of spiking neurons, in order not to induce unwanted connections between the indicators for Brown and Black, or between those for Horse and Black, Blanket and Brown, and Horse and Blanket.

The two constituents then activate the respective sensorial concepts and the phenomenally dedicated neurons in the visual system, such that a situation of a brown horse and a black blanket can be imagined, or recognized in perception.

A remembrance of a situation with a brown horse and a black horse, and likewise the phrase *a black horse and a brown horse*, would be organized from out the memory indices such that the two different indices are both connected to the Horse-indicator and are connected to the Brown-, and the Black-indicator, respectively.

We see that the concept indicator for horses is connected with two different indices for individuals in M, one is in circuit activation with the indicators for Black and Horse, and the other with the indicators for Brown and Horse. The circuits should be in different phases.

On the other hand, a remembrance of a black and brown horse, and likewise the phrase *a black and brown horse*, would be organized from out the memory by a single index since only a single individual is involved, as shown in Figure 7. Here, since organized from out a single index, the circuits are in the same phase of neuron firing, whereby an incidental connection between the

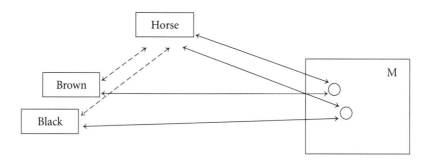

Figure 6. Memory activation of the episode "A black horse and a brown horse"

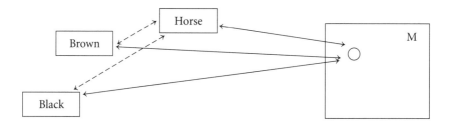

Figure 7. Memory activation of the episode: A black and brown horse

indicators for Black and for Brown can be induced in relation to the indicator for Horse.

As far as Figure 7 goes, this structure of activation circuits is an indicator for every possibly remembered situation in which there is a black and brown horse. The remembered episode is a particular one by the specific place of the index within the spatial, temporal and causal contiguity order between indices in the episodic memory base M. This order can be established by connections the indices have with indicators of spatial, temporal, and causal order. If the remembrance is more detailed, for example that the horse's tail was brown and the head was black, then the indicator of the remembered situation would be more complex by having the indicators for horse-tails and for horse-heads and the indicators for their positional relations within the whole body of a horse activated in circuits also along connections with the indicators for brown and black, respectively. The structuring of a remembered episode from out the memory indices follows, in the case of reliable remembrance, the way in which the original episode was structured as a perceived situation, or they are built up in understanding a description and interpreting it in the world or some model. These structures are the same for perceptions as well as for images.

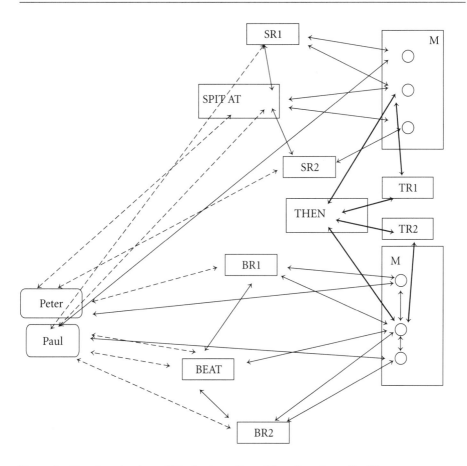

Figure 8. Circuit activation of "Paul spits at Peter. Then Peter beats Paul."

Via the situation index, namely the index for the event or action or process, which is the middle index in Figure 4, connected with the indicator for the general concept Beat, the situation can be related to other situations. Likewise this indicator can be used for further characterizations of the action, which in language are expressed by adverbial constructions of different kinds. Figure 8 presents the circuit activation for remembering a scene with two basic situations or episodes in temporal order. The solid arrows represent connections that are fixed in memory. When they get activated from out the indices they can induce temporarily the weakly dotted connections.

TR1 and TR2 indicate the roles of 'Before' and 'After' in the temporal relationship of succession indicated by THEN. SR1 and SR2 indicate the role concepts of the one who spits and of the one who is pitted at, respectively.

Likewise, BR1 and BR2 indicate the concepts of the roles of the beater and the beaten one, respectively.

This all has been explicated to this degree in order to oppose criticism on connectionist neurological modeling, as it has been put forward by linguists in the mentalist tradition.

Jackendoff (2002: 58–66), in his criticism on current neuro-science as not being able to show "how neurons instantiate the details of rules of grammar" (p. 58), has used examples with linguistic structures like the ones treated above as examples that could not be functionally explained by current models of neuro-science. The problem of binding concepts within constituents cannot be solved by just referring to spreading activation and rhythmic firing of groups of neurons. He is, of course, right in this criticism. The same problem had also been pointed out in Bartsch (2002: Chapter 2), where it had been shown that and why simple connectionist neural networks cannot deal sufficiently with binding, compositionality, and inference. To remedy this deficiency of connectionist models, the architecture of circuit activation was introduced, which permits to have smaller circuits embedded into larger ones, corresponding to semantically motivated constituents in situations and all kinds of representations, such as pictures, images, perceptions, and inscriptions of sentences. The present essay extends and elaborates this principle of circuit activation by including the memory as a capacity of constructing remembrances.

Findings and modeling of circuitry in the prefrontal cortex, other cortical regions, the para-hippocampal region and the hippocampus, and direct and indirect pathways between these areas and via the nucleus reunions have been reported and shown in their importance for the overall memory functions by Witter et al. (1989) and by Dalatour and Witter (2002), and in further work by these authors, which investigates the organization of memory performed by the whole cortico-hippocampal system, the thalamus, and the amygdala. The interactions between these systems support the model of the role of memory in understanding, as it is explored on the phenomenological and semantic level on the one hand side, and by the semantically motivated connectionist-neural architecture on the other. The situation with respect to constituent structure and binding, and with respect to the role of the working memory and episodic memory is thus much better than Jackendoff (2002) assumes. There is a semantically motivated model, the present one, which is supported in its principles by findings of neuro-science.

Remembering is a special act of imagination, namely one determined by indices in the episodic memory area **M**. Phenomenologically, this amounts to the imagination being embedded within one's history, i.e. within the autobiographical memory, and hereby the image is understood as a remembered episode, and not just as a free fantasy. Remembering and imagining are often hard to distinguish, because remembering can include parts that were not present in the original episode, but come from other remembered episodes, or are added from cross-activation with and among conceptual indicators on the ontological conceptual maps and on the categorizing maps of the sensorial modalities and of the motor and emotional maps. Imagination for a large part can be understood as free combination of reconstructed parts of episodes indexed in area **M**. Thus memory plays an essential part as a basis for employing the power of imagination, also in our present experience of situations. We shall see in Proust's *A la Recherche du Temps Perdu* how, for example, the feelings of love, jealousy, and fear of being forsaken are transferred on situations later in the life of the Narrator from out the basic scene in which his mother refuses to come up to his room for a good night kiss, because she has to entertain dinner guests. The episodes in the same line are situations of his early relationships to his grandmother, to Gilberte, and then to Albertine. They are paralleled by the love and jealousy of Swann with respect to Odette. All these situations experienced by the Narrator or by Swann can partially be mapped on each other in essential, that is repeating, aspects, and they imply similar emotions and attitudes. The old episodes are re-lived in the new ones in modified forms.

3.   The architecture of remembrance and deficiencies of memory

In what follows I shall report on some memory deficiencies attended to in the neurological and psychiatric literature. This I do in order to show properties of the architecture of remembering by contrasting the deficient cases with the normal ones and explaining what necessary part of the architecture may be missing by anatomical or physiological reasons, causing the deficiency.

The Russian neurologist and psychologist Luria reported about the case of the soldier Zazjetski, who became one of his patients after a severe head wound, which he had received in the war. There were parts of his brain damaged, which made that his memory about episodes that he had experienced during his life was very peculiar. He reported about the episodes not from his own perspective and involvement, rather he described them as if they had happened to a stranger. He did not understand his reports as being about himself and what he had experienced. He even did not remember that he personally had experienced these episodes. He had no emotional involvement in them and did not use any self-centered deictic descriptions of the episodes. He, as a person (as the I-person) was totally absent in his reports. He still understood his own reports as factual about the soldier Zazjetski, and he could imagine the scenes reported like one can imagine scenes described in any storybook. The episodes to him were not part of his life-history. In fact, as far as he was concerned, he had no life-history anymore, though he could report on what had happened to a third person. His episodic memory, we can say, did not function as an autobiographic memory, though merely as a fact memory.

Our first question is how that fits into the sketch of episodic memory given above. Apparently the connections of area **M** to the conceptual maps and to the sensorial maps were still intact, as were these areas. He still could perceive and imagine episodes. He also could realize himself as a third person being part of an episode and could also imagine this being so. But he could not remember this having been so for himself. What must have been damaged were the connections of area **M** to the proprioception areas of own motion, directedness, intention, evaluation, and especially emotion, as well as bodily feelings involved in self-perception. The area that is essential for emotional involvement is the amygdala, which is located at both sides of the brain right under the hippocampus, the area **M** of episodic memory, where I assume that the neurons are located which function as memory indices. Possibly the amygdala itself was damaged, or at least its connections to the hippocampus.

The second question is a conceptual and phenomenological one: Would we want to call the ability of recollection shown by soldier Zazjetski 'remembering'? He does not even know that he really remembers something he personally has experienced. He wouldn't say "I remember that … happened to me". He knows events, such that there was a war; he knows that soldier Zazjetski got wounded at his head. He does not remember what that meant to him. He knows how to tell stories, while at the same time being able to understand his stories as reports about some events that have happened in the world. He can imagine what these events are like, and he can imagine what they would be like for others. Objectively speaking, he does recollect episodes he had experienced. He can understand reports and he can distinguish facts from fantasy, since he reports facts and not fantasy. But he cannot make this distinction by arguing that something is a fact because he has personally experienced it. It is a fact because it is reported, when being ask to give a report. We want to say that certainly facts are recollected by this individual's memory, i.e. by connective activity including area **M**, conceptual maps, and sensorial maps), while at the same time the episodes that establish these facts for the individual are not remembered as episodes he as an "I" had part in. In recollecting the facts he partly imagines the events that support these, though without himself being part of the episodes, not as a participant and not as an experiencer. It is a deficient way of remembering; it is not remembering in the way in which our remembrances make up our life-history. We can say that this is a partial recollection, a fact recollection, without remembering. Remembrance includes the experience of the I-person, while recollection is just a recollection of some facts.

Squire and Kandel (2000) report about William Scoville's and Brenda Milner's observation that a patient in whom the hippocampus-area had been eliminated by an operation was, from then on, no more able to keep episodes in long-term memory, though he had understood them and shortly held them in his short-term memory. Nevertheless the patient was able to remember several episodes from his life before the operation. How is this possible? An explanation would be that those were episodes he previously had remembered several times in thinking about them, or talking about them. Because of this repetition of the circuit activation between the conceptual indicators involved and the sensorial and pre-motor fields while re-imagining the previous episode and possibly formulating repeatedly a linguistic representation of it, the episode got generalized in the sense that it became part of the general semantic memory. From there it can be remembered, like we can imagine an example for whatever general concept of which we have established a conceptual indicator in terms of an activation pattern that can be called up by some appropriate linguistic input or some similar situational input.

In order to form an instance, an example, for a general concept of a situation, there should be an area in which indices get temporarily created, serving for organizing the situation or episode in binding together the involved conceptual indicators and indices of the individual concepts involved, such that the evolving structure of activation circuits can be used in an act of reference to a possible satisfaction situation. These temporal indices then cannot induce indices for long term memory in the memory area **M**, if the hippocampus is missing. In such a case there then is no way to remember episodes over a longer time. The indices for the short-term memory of a situation, used in understanding a situation or a sentence, might be located in the prefrontal cortex according to the findings of Raffone and Wolters (2001), who locate the maintenance function and the control function of the working memory in this area. That there is a short-term memory possible without a long-term memory just means that as long as we attend to a situation or to a linguistic input by thinking about it and exploring it, the circuit activation between the involved conceptual indicators and sensorial and pre-motor fields is going on. These circuits die out when the attention is shifted to a new episode or linguistic utterance, and without the mediating function of the hippocampus area nothing of the episode could be fixed in the so-called episodic, or declarative memory. This also explains the case of Damasio's patient David, reported about below.

There are further memory deficiencies and abnormalities of different kinds, which can be explained by the above model of the architecture of memory and the process of remembering. There are also observations concerning the normal capacity of remembering which fit into this model. I shall start with the latter.

Draaisma (2001) gives a historical overview about the explanations of the fact that we do not remember episodes from our early years of childhood, including most of the first three or four years. Some things that we seem to remember later in life are based on stories told about noteworthy episodes from our early childhood, for example when looking at older photographs together with older family members.

The best explanation of the memory gap of the early years is the one that claims that in order to remember something for a longer time, we first have to develop general concepts and routines by repetition of episodes, perception of objects and own and others actions and activities. We have seen above that the memory needs these general concepts for constructing remembrances. A further explication of this explanation is that early memories become part of the general process of generalization and schematization, which by linguistic guidance slowly becomes stabilized to the conceptualizations more in the line with the way the grown-ups interpret situations. The first, still unstable ways of ordering experiences, which made for the early interpretations of perceptual and motor data, have got replaced in the ongoing learning processes by the later orderings, constituting the adult conceptual system. Since in the above model of memory the memory indices of area **M** are meaningful merely by their connections to the conceptual indicators on the conceptual maps, the indices become useless if they lose their previous connections with earlier, not yet stabilized and thus tentative indicators of concepts of actions, events, and objects. This of course happens as long as these concept and routine indicating neuronal assemblies are still unstable in their location, extension, and relationships to other conceptual indicators on conceptual maps, motor maps, and sensorial maps. Likewise, episodes are no more remembered when the necessary conceptual indicators, or their connections with the memory indices got destroyed. Thus, without generalizing memory there is no episodic memory, as our model of the constructive memory predicts.

Another explanation reported by Draaisma is the one which points out that for an autobiographic memory to be possible, the child first has to develop self-consciousness; it has to recognize itself not just as the one whom it sees in the mirror, which happens around the age of 12 months; rather the child has to understand itself as integrating its experienced episodes in a history, which is its own history, in which certain episodes have another emotional value than they have for the other participants of these episodes. The last point requires that the child has some ideas about the psychology of other people, which develop about the age of three. This explanation refers to the connections of the indices in area M, the hippocampus, with the indicators of the proprioceptional and emotional organization of the self via the amygdala. These indicators are generalizations and stand in contiguity orderings of bodily feelings and emotions. The two explanations are certainly compatible, i.e. they can be true at the same time, and they both fit well within the architecture of memory.

Haberlandt (1999:226), referring to Bruner and Feldman, writes that "the autobiographical narrative provides a framework for making sense of events and for telling them to someone else ... the narrative is held together by the person's view of self... the narrative does preserve essential events as they were experienced, but it is not a factual report; rather the account seeks to make a certain point, to unify events, or to justify them." The episodic memory is the basis of the autobiographical narrative. It serves to make a schema of the self, to become conscious of one's wishes and expectations. Haberlandt points out that the autobiographic memory and its narratives are social creations – "they are shared with as well as shaped by other people" (1999:227). Referring to Barclay, he writes that the autobiographic memories define a person's self relative to others. The narrative of self gives continuity and meaning to a person's life." (1999:228). Haberlandt also remarks, that "as a result of reflection and new circumstances many recollections do change as the years go by" (1999:227). This fact of change of memory over time, of course, is very well compatible with the assumption of a constructive memory. It would not be compatible with a memory that was a stock of ready made representations of some kind.

Another not unusual case of remembering discussed by Draaisma (2001) is the activation of memory in extremo: near-death experiences. During, and directly after, an unsolicited fall, or when nearly drowning, or in situations of being close to dying, many people, in a fast sequence or in a kind of vast panorama view, remember scenes from their life-history in a detailed manner and in a serene and happy way. The best explanation given in the literature about these phenomena rests on two facts. First, in such an extreme situation, there are hardly any sensorial stimuli, especially no visual stimuli or bodily feelings such as pain, because the transmission from the sensors to the brain is not working anymore, though sometimes a sound can still be heard. Secondly, endorphins are massively produced in the brain, which enhance the capacity of neural transmission and especially cause feelings of happiness and serenity. The sensorial fields and the proprioceptual fields are not occupied by perceptual activity and thus they are all free to work for the imaginations and hallucinations woken up by activation of the emotional, conceptual, and motor areas of the brain, including areas of imaginary self-representation. When these activate the memory indices in area **M**, this results in remembering rapidly the scenes from the past. Without involvement of area **M** we just get very vivid hallucinations, which are also frequently reported, not only in near-death experiences but also in cases of being doped by morphine or opium.

Draaisma (2001) reports that the amount of available associations makes for a strong memory restricted to certain fields of expertise, for example in playing chess, where the expert knows many specific contiguity relationships he had experienced previously between a situation and possible constellations, and then can remember positions on many chess boards by having them available via the generalizations over contiguity relationships between positions and moves, which he has formed as a system of concepts of positions or patterns, and routines. Here a specific concrete position of one of the many boards on which the master plays against other players simultaneously is embedded in a certain conceptualization, including a routine. This means for our model that the memory indices in **M** are established in connection with this conceptualization and can easily be remembered from out the respective concept indicators, which also imply the call-up of the appropriate routine. A very unusual, stupid and totally unexpected move and a position thus resulting, which does not fit in any pattern, cannot be remembered in this way, rather merely via the emotional experience of astonishment, if there had been time to stick to that situation for a little while. In our model we can explain this situation like this: Relating the emotion to the face of the player, the move and position may be remembered when the emotional activation connects to the indices of the move or position, and they then connect to the indicators of the visual and motor concept describing it. The exceptional situation is characterized on this lower sensorial and motor level and not in the higher conceptual level of constellations and routines.

That constellations or patterns that were experienced and first encoded with the help of hippocampal functions get consolidated over time by replaying them in reality or in imagination, or even unconsciously while sleeping, has been shown in rat-experiments by Morris's (2003) research on memory consolidation. Here 16 days after learning to identify a certain location, coupled with an event of reward, the hippocampus of the rat was removed, but the rat was still able to find its way to the place and get the reward, while it lost this capability if the hippocampus was removed shortly after the learn-ing process. Memory is consolidated over time, and in our terms, we can say that episodes, which are replayed, get generalized to situational concepts, and thus get established their own conceptual indicator on the cortex by the cir-cuit activation between the hippocampal indices and the conceptual indicators involved, and their induced interaction circuits. A chess player replays an expe-rienced constellation, an episode, and thus gets induced a conceptual indicator, and its interrelationships with other conceptual indicators of constellations, in his general memory, outside the hippocampus. This then is activated when he sees a new instance of the constellation, and he can act immediately.

The last cases reported by Draaisma (2001), which I want to discuss, are the ones of autistic patients and other so-called savants. These are people who have unusually highly developed abilities in a very narrow field of activity, while per-forming very low in other areas. These people, for example, find their way in a calendar reaching over hundreds of years, which they somehow have stored in their memory in such a way that they exactly can tell which day of the week is a certain date long ago, or in the far away future. Other such people know the bus and train schedules of a whole city or country by hart, others can per-form complicated mathematical operations on huge numbers without paper and pencil, and others, again, can play every piece of music which they have heard once on the piano, without knowing any notes.

Luria's patient Sherashevsky was one of those who could remember sur-prisingly complex mathematical formulas, without understanding them. He could remember long lists of more than 50 or 70 or even 100 numbers, letters, words, and none-sense syllables. This phenomenon is called an absolute mem-ory. It seems to be isolated from thinking and from generalizations and more abstract conceptualization. Sherashevsky could remember masses of uncon-nected details, but had no feeling for theories and higher conceptual orderings. Everything he remembered he presented on the level of lower, fairly specific, general experiential concepts and the experiential contiguity order within and between small scenes. He described scenes and episodes very vividly and clear in every detail. Hereby a special capacity was his syn-aesthetic experience. Sounds were for him connected with visual and haptic sensations, such that he characterized the sound of a specific voice as yellow and granular. What he saw he also experienced in terms of taste, smell, touch, and sound sensations, and the same happened with what he heard, whereby he also had visual, taste, smell, and touch sensations. For him a visual experience in memory was connected with experiences in the other modalities, and in this way it could be accessed from all these different angles in remembering. The many associations from all the different sensorial modalities made it possible for him to remember situations with masses of details. In terms of our model of constructive memory we can say that the indices in the M-area were established in connection with many different low-level concepts, especially in connection with those of the different sensorial modalities. Thus one index may be an index connected with a conceptual indicator for a kind of visual experience, sound experience, touch experience and/or smell experience. Thus the index also is multiple accessible from out all these kinds of sensations. The disadvantage of this special capacity of syn-aesthetic experience is, of course, an overload of experiential detail, and we can expect that with all these neuronal activations present in perceiving a situation, there is not much energy available (in terms of neurotransmitters and what else to be produced) for getting activated the higher neuronal circuits that are necessary for more abstract and theoretical thinking, and for getting them re-activated when they have been established as permanent dispositions. His very special and highly developed capacity in remembering perceived details in fact resulted in a weakness in performing the higher cognitive functions. We can summarize his condition as living in a multi-modality, impressionist world. This is an impressionist world consisting of impressions formed by the different sensory modalities and strong connections between them. We find this emphasis on sensations and impressions in the description of many scenes in Proust's *A la Recherche du temps perdu*.

Damasio (1999) reports about his patient David, who after encephalitis has a total loss of specific memory. He still conceptualizes correctly according to general semantic categories. Thus he does not know who a certain person is he has talked with often, or even ten minutes ago, but he categorizes him as a friend, or as someone to dislike on the basis of emotional expressions and behavior he presently observes on the person. He also cannot identify places or scenes, though he can characterize them in general terms. His memory is restricted to a short time memory of 45 seconds. As he is able to apply general concepts, he also is able to apply routines and general rules of behavior. But he is not able to recognize specific social relationships as those that have been established previously. It is interesting that he also is not able to plan events and actions beforehand, which requires imagination and memory of imagined episodes. Apparently, this ability would require the temporal-local organization which can be fixed by indices in the specific, episodic memory area and which would make future courses of events constructible in analogy with previously experienced courses of events.

4.   The role of memory in understanding

What now is the function of memory in understanding? Memory induces expectations. In perceiving a situation or object, the received sensorial information gets understood by activating connections to indicators for similar information experienced previously, which are indicators of ontological categories, emotional categories, motor routines. From there activation comes back to the sensorial areas via reciprocal connections, which re-activates or strengthens the activation of the neurons primarily stimulated, and also activates further neurons, which are then especially receptive for further information from the situation, or even provide imagined expected information about the situation. If the situation provides this expected information then the categorization from out the conceptual maps is strengthened. There can be alternative activation circuits between the sensorial and the conceptual maps; the ones that come out strongest by this process of reinforcement between conceptual activation and sensorial activation from receiving input will be the final result of understanding, the 'interpretation' or 'conceptualization' of the situation as such and such a situation. This all is done by the general memory including the semantic memory and routines, and the reinforcement its categorizations get by further received data from the situation or object. Expectation can be re-enforced, or can be disappointed in perceiving contrasting evidence.

Additionally the specific or episodic memory also contributes to understanding a situation. The specific internal and external space-time ordering of the situation is partially indicated by ordering of the received input on the primary sensorial fields, which gets fixed by activation of indicators of general concepts of spatial and temporal order, and by activation returning from there to the sensorial fields. The indicators of concepts of spatial and temporal order activate via connections some indices in the specific memory area, as do also the general indicators of ontological, emotional, and routine categories. Those groups of indices activated strongest by adding up the activation from all the different sources stand for the situation previously experienced that is most similar to the present situation, or they stand for a composition of aspects of situations that are most similar to the present one under different respects. Thus the newly experienced situation is perceived and understood as something that is similar to a specific, previously experienced situation. The emotion and action potential and the proprioceptional experience of this previous situation, and its space-time and causal contiguity relationships to other specific situations now become available as previous experience, which guides how one personally manages the new situation. This belongs to understanding the new situation in a broader sense, not just as categorizing it but also as giving rise to a certain handling of the situation. It is recognition of something old in something new, activating previously accompanying action-patterns and emotional re-actions.

The episode activated in memory need not to be really remembered, that is become emergent in consciousness by getting into a connecting circuit activation with the sensory-motor fields. It will not become conscious as a whole episode, if the presently perceived situation strongly occupies the sensory-motor capacities to such an extent that the previous episode activated in the specific and general memory cannot as a whole form circuit activation with the sensory-motor and emotional fields. Although there is no remembrance in this case, there still can be influence on understanding the present situation, enacted from the indicators involved within the memory activity. In this case there is no conscious comparison between the present situation and the previous episode.

In this context, we may ask ourselves how retrieval of a previous situation and encoding of the new situation that is partially identical with the previous one do not get mixed up thus that the present perception is totally distorted. Hasselmo et al. (2002) has modeled the role of the theta rhythm of the hippocampus and the prefrontal cortex of a virtual rat that learned a certain path to a source of food. Then the source of food was placed at the other side such that the previously successful path was reversed into the other direction in its second part. The rat had in the end to make a distinction between the remembered path and the new path. The two different phases, up and down, of the theta rhythm served to separate retrieval of the old situation from encoding the new situation. When the theta rhythm was suppressed, the rat was not able to encode the new path, but got totally mixed up about the two paths. The model, in which neural spiking and synaptic plasticity, and theta rhythm was modeled, all in relationship with mouse behavior, also showed how retrieval can be context-dependent: the rat learned alternations in the path when the alternations where placed within a sequence with running a left or a right circle in a maze.

Based on phenomenological data, experiences we have of ourselves and others, we can assume that the specific, historical, memory can also contribute to enforcing one activation circuit of understanding above other alternative ones and thus can influence the choice of the most appropriate or preferred 'interpretation' of received sensorial activation. The understanding is then most appropriate, not just according to general conceptual understanding through categories, rather according to maybe a singular emotionally very involving personal experience in the past. The latter might even overrule the strongest activation circuit of general understanding and reinforce a weaker one, which in conceptual characterization is less adequate, but is favored by a strong emotion and action routine, via the specific episodic memory. In this way the understanding of a situation becomes very biased, due to a previously experienced episode with a strong emotional involvement. This happens in the examples mentioned from Proust's *A la recherche du temps perdu*, where feelings of love, jealousy, and being left alone, developed in early childhood interaction with the narrator's mother, lead to favored ways of understanding, i.e. conceptualizing, of situations later in life, and to re-actions to later situations of interaction with the women he loves. In this way also certain individual concepts we have formed can function a role-models for our behavior in certain types of situations, where we follow these role-models that we have seen in earlier situations and to which we are emotionally attached.

CHAPTER 3

Concept formation, remembrance, and understanding

The origin of this chapter has been the theory of concept formation and understanding in *Dynamic Conceptual Semantics* (Bartsch 1998) and the work on consciousness, memory, perception, and action in *Consciousness Emerging* (Bartsch 2002). When then re-reading Proust's *A la recherche du temps perdu* I was surprised about how much of Proust's novel, or rather series of novels, conforms to the principles and structures of concept formation and understanding, and the role of memory in perception and action. When afterwards Bergson's book on matter and memory was brought to my attention, which was written and published at a time when Proust had just started out on writing his novels, I read Bergson in order to find out whether Proust's ideas about memory, perception, action, and understanding, and his design of the structure of his novel, as well as the elaboration of episodes might be based on what Bergson had to say on these topics.

1. Bergson and Proust

Proust had followed Bergson's lectures around 1900 and he continued to keep in incidental contact with Bergson not only via his family ties – Bergson was married to a second cousin of Proust's – but also by meeting him in the salons he frequented and in the committees for prizes in literature and the arts and cultural affairs, in which both now and then took part (George D. Painter [1983/1959], *Marcel Proust. A Biography*).

The biographer Tadié writes (2001:127) that 'on 7 January 1892 Proust's path crossed that of a man with whom he would often be compared: Henri Bergson. Marcel had been page-boy at the wedding of his cousin Louise Neuburger to the philosopher.' They were not close and had little contact with each other. Both insisted on being very distinct from each other in outlook, ideas, and method. Proust had read Bergson's *Matière et mémoire*. However, he

pointed out that his approach to memory was quite different from Bergson's
(Tadié 2002:128). Above all it may have been their resemblance that drew
them apart:

> Bergson did not like to be preceded by anyone or questioned, and he preferred
> to be left alone by friends or colleagues. Scarcely lavish in his use of footnotes
> in his books, he occasionally inserted them in order to indicate his indepen-
> dent position with regard to those doctrines that one might absent-mindedly
> compare to his.

Similarly Proust, when he read *Matiere et mémoire*, took note of their different
approaches, and, in an interview, refused to allow *Swann* to be labeled as a
'Bergsonian novel'.

According to Tadié, Proust had stated that 'the distinction between voluntary and involuntary memory dominated all his work, whereas this did not
feature in Bergson's philosophy, and was even contradicted by it.'

This last is not true. Also for Bergson, the influence of the memory on
perception is always involuntary. Besides this, there is remembrance, which can
come up in two ways, voluntarily or involuntarily. However, this is not a matter
of discussion for Bergson. For Proust, of course, the involuntary remembrance
is that which causes aesthetic pleasure, and thus is in the center of his interest,
while voluntarily called up remembrances do not have this special quality. This
point will be dealt with in the section on Proust.

Indeed, Bergson's philosophy on matter and memory contains the main
ideas we find described, reflected on, and worked out in the structure and
the details of Proust's novel. Bergson's philosophy on memory has also much
in common with the theory on concept formation and understanding presented in Bartsch (1998, 2002), namely the experientially and contextually
based structuralist model of concept formation, and the relationships with
neuro-physiological and psychological findings. Bergson, in *On Memory and
Matter*, combines Phenomenological Philosophy with Psychology and also
neurological findings of his time. In his work we find the beginnings of neuro-
psychology, as we know it today. In order to see these relationships, it is in-
structive to start out this essay with a short report on the work by Bergson on
matter and memory, which had been translated soon after its publication by
the German neo-Kantian Wilhelm Windelband: Bergson (1908), Materie und
Gedächtnis.

I shall refer to this German translation as the source for the following pages.

2.   Bergson on memory, perception, action, and understanding

Bergson first tries to show how our intuition of space arises from embedding sensorial information into motor and pre-motor activity. This he formulates in the way that bodily activity and our potential for action is essential for perceiving spatial relationships. Sensorial images arise by having sensorial input related to centers of activity of a living being and getting it organized and understood from out these activities and their requirements. He writes (1908: 54–55) that visual space and haptic space are united by motor activity. Our intuition of spatial and temporal extension is potential activity, pre-motor activity in the brain.

When trying to answer the question of how consciousness can come about from internal movements of the brain he recurs to the role of memory in perceiving and understanding. He writes:

> There is no perception that is not saturated by memories. We intermingle our present sensory impressions with thousands of details of previous experiences. Mostly these remembrances replace our immediate sensorial input, which is reduced to some hints, to mere tokens, which remind us on old images. This is a necessary condition for the easy functioning of perception; but it also is the source of all kinds of illusions (1908: 20). Even though a perception to us seems to be short, it still takes some time and requires an inset of the memory, which merges several sequential moments into a unity. Even the 'subjectivity' of the sensorial qualities consists, as we want to show, mainly in a manner of contracting what is real by means of our memory. In short, the memory forms in two ways the main part of our individual consciousness in perception, first by weaving the immediate sensorial input into a network of remembrances, and second by contracting a plurality of moments.   (1908: 19. Translation mine)

Here Bergson mentions the two kinds of memory, first the specific, episodic memory organized by contiguity relationships of spatial, temporal, causal, and motivational kind, and second the generalizing (semantic) memory, which binds the sensory impressions conceptually into one thing, or situation, or constellation of situations. We have argued in the previous chapter that this happens by means of a concept indicator. The selection of reactions of the body on the stimulations by objects and other bodies is determined by our previous experiences; the reactions do not take place without re-activating remembrances, relicts of analog events and processes. It is clear that the amount of momentary real sensory impression on which our perception of the external world is built, is small compared with what the memory adds to it (1908: 56). And there is also no capturing the future without an equal, respective look backwards into the past (1908: 56). This means that in planning and newly experiencing we make use of our memory, the general memory of concepts and routines, as well as the specific memory of individuals, episodes, and historically ordered courses of events.

Bergson still seems to adhere partly to what we now take as the traditional cognitive position in that he assumes internal images which are not presently perceived, but which are stored in memory. These are images that form our past, i.e. the reality we have experienced previously. He distinguishes a memory based on images of repeated experiences and a memory of re-imagined, specific, episodic images, which are integrated by contiguity relationships with surrounding episodes and especially actions. In the first, repeating memory we can distinguish general images based on repeated perceptions and generalizations of repeated actions, routines. The re-imagining memory follows the general repeating memory when it provides repeated images for the re-imagining memory, initiated by sensorial input, actions and routines. However, images are not simply stored. In the imagining memory the image gets re-designed (1908: 82–83). The remembered episode is not just a ready image, but a re-construction, which explains that the remembrances are reproductions that are not always true in every detail. Thus Bergson already envisaged a constructive memory, though he also used the old metaphor of the memory as a store of images.

Proust's novel is full of such episodes that are produced in imagination by the interaction of current situational impressions and remembrances: A new experience always also is an old experience; a new action is a somewhat modified repetition of an old action. Habits and concepts are formed from early childhood on and permeate the experiences and actions of the adult. They play an organizing role in the entire life-history of a person.

Bergson takes "reality for us" as consisting of clusters of images ordered around our past and present activities. Our perception and our past and present reality are reduced to that which is of interest to us. A separate representation, an imagination, is the extraction or isolation of an image from the contiguity of images in which it finds its continuation. The contiguity creates our consciousness of the reality of a perception (1908: 22). Consciousness of a perception consists in the reflection of the objects at the self of the observer. In this process the objects (in distinction to the thing in itself) lose something, but also gain something from the self of the observer. Consciousness consists in the selection of aspects from the object in perception, and this selection takes place according to possibilities of action of the body with respect to the object. The ability of discrimination is organized in this manner (1908: 24). In this way there is a unity of object and observer in perception, where the interaction of the observer with the object takes place. A hallucination is not an isolated representation in the brain, rather it receives the illusion of reality by being embedded into the activity of memory (1908: 30), and we want to add, this happens in being embedded into the contiguity of present perceptions and activities.

The role of bodily activity in organizing perception and the function of memory means that our perception includes the motor centers in our brain. Even though perception is guided by what the sensory nerves transmit, it has as a whole its cause in the tendency of our body towards movement (1908: 32–33). Our senses receive some education in learning processes towards co-ordination and filling in the gaps between the separate sensory take-ups in order to achieve an overall picture of an object. The several aspects are bound together into the unity of an object and into a unity with the movement or activity (1908: 36). We see here the unity of the object achieved by the categorization or conceptualization of the object, which is dependent on the unity according to the special contiguity of the object with activities related to it. The selection of aspects for categorizing the object, and herewith our consciousness of the object under a certain characterization, is caused by possible movements and at the same time consciously aims at the actions involving these movements. In conformity with what is said above, Bergson sees the experience of the external formed by the living body as a centre, from which that is reflected on the surrounding objects what (generally) is the effect of these objects on this body. The perception of the external consists in this reflection (1908: 45).

Affections such as pain are local motor reactions of the body to stimulations. Sensory impressions in extremo become painful, for example sensing extremely strong light, heat, or sound (1908: 48–49). On the other hand, pleasure can be felt by soft, soothing, harmonic, rhythmic stimulation of the body in perception, causing local motor reactions that are pleasant. Proust exploits this fact repeatedly in *A la recherche* when he describes the affections caused by his mother's good night kiss, the moving pictures along the wall of his bedroom projected by the magic lantern, the moving steeples of the churches when driving through the hilly county around Combray, the smells and colors of the flowers, trees, and bushes, their enchanting composition with ponds, creeks, and along riversides, experienced on the walks through gardens and countryside, the little musical phrase in the sonata by Vinteuil, played by Odette, and also by Albertine, the typical phrases in Bergotte's books. The affections that had been caused by these experiences are the hinges for remembering these scenes in later courses of life.

Recognition is the process in which past and present embrace each other. In the experience of recognition, perception and remembrance merge into each other. In recognizing a place or an object, the recollection of an image is connected with courses of actions or movements.

Places such as Combray, Balbec, Paris, in Proust's novel are recognized repeatedly by taking the same walks. A place is known by walking through it and around it, in reality and in imagination. Also persons are recognized and familiar by playing a role in repeated actions, routines or habits of the Narrator. As a child, the Narrator walks quite a lot with his grandmother in Combray, in Balbec, and in Paris. As a youth the Narrator gets familiar with girls and women by walking in the same places: with Gilberte by repeated walks in the Champs-Elysées, later with Albertine by repeated walks and trips by motor car or train in and around Balbec, and then with the Duchesse de Guermantes by walking certain streets and places in Paris. All these habitual walks are the actions in which he is affected by love, a pleasure which is heightened when he recognizes the respective person.

There are several examples in *A la recherche* where an action or bodily event causes a remembrance, even leading to an illusion (Vol. 3:716): "And once, when I had said good night to Gilberte rather early, I woke up in the middle of the night in my room at Tansonville and, still half asleep, called out "Albertine!" It was not that I had thought of her or dreamt of her, not that I was confusing her with Gilberte, but a memory in my arm, opening like a flower, had made me fumble behind my bed for the bell, as though I had been in my bed-room in Paris. And not finding it, I had called out: "Albertine!", thinking that my dead mistress was lying by my side, as she had often done in the evening, and that we were both dropping off to sleep, and reckoning, as I woke up, that, because of the time it would take Francoise to reach my room, Albertine might without imprudence pull the bell which I could not find." Another example of the connection of bodily movement with the episodic memory is the Narrator's tripping against an uneven paving stone in the court-yard of the Guermantes mansion, which was like the tripping on the uneven paving stones in the baptistery of the St. Marcus in Venice, and hereby called up the remembrance of his visit in Venice a long time ago (Vol. 3:898).

Recognition is not possible without embedding what is present into contiguity with these movements. Apraxia is a deficiency where a person is unable to recognize anything. He still makes use of the general repeated memory without this embedding, i.e. such a person is able to conceptualize and thus to perceive in general terms, without this embedding into own movements and action. According to Bergson the familiarity is to be found in the well-organized accompanying movements. In this way well-known objects and instruments, but also persons, are recognized: the perception is continued in action. This recognition of individual objects, but also of kinds of objects, means that they are integrated into a practice of the observer. Bergson thus distinguishes a distanced objective categorization from recognition.

We shall see in the following section on Proust, that the embedding of a remembrance into a current episode of a perception, a bodily feeling, or a movement makes the remembrance be rooted in actual reality, and in this way it feels to be real, part of the actual, and thus appears recognized rather than imagined. The cognitive and at the same time aesthetic pleasure felt with such a remembrance is the pleasure of recognition of something one is acquainted with; it is recognition of the old within the new. And this is something involuntary, as recognition generally happens involuntarily, also in Bergson's writings on memory.

As has been mentioned above, the education of the senses consists in the whole of connections between a sensory impression and the movement which makes use of this impression. Proportional to the number of repetitions of the impression the connection gets stronger. Bergson compares this relationship to a tune, where one note already bends itself to the next note (1908: 89). The dependence of an impression on the relevant action is a special kind of context-dependence. He elaborates this essential relationship of impression and action further: Like every normal experience has its organized accompanying motor activity, the feeling of recognition has its roots in the becoming conscious of this organization. This means that we generally play the recognition before we think it. Our daily life takes place between objects, the mere presence of which invites us to play a role: their familiarity consists in this invitation (1908: 89).

In *A la Recherche* we see the Narrator playing his different roles in the company of his great-aunt Leonie, his grandmother, his mother, Odette (Mme Swann), Mme Verdurin, the Duchesse de Guermantes, Gilberte, and Albertine, and others, and we see how his role changes with the changes of these persons; they become different persons to him in the course of time, and so his behavior and role changes with respect to them. But also he changes and so the persons and also the places change with respect to him. Tansonville, Swann's country-place at Combray, and the walks around Combray are not the same to the Narrator when he stays there during the war with Gilberte, then married to Saint-Loup. The affections are lost; he is disenchanted with the scenes of his youth (Vol. 3: 710): "But separated as I was by a whole lifetime from places I now happened to be passing through again, there was lacking between them and me that contiguity from which is born, even before we have perceived it, the immediate, delicious and total deflagration of memory. Having doubtless no very clear conception of its nature, I was saddened by the thought that my faculty of feeling and imagining things must have diminished since I no longer took any pleasure in these walks." The mysteries of his childhood were no more there. Then the Guermantes had been unreachable from out his social sphere, the glass-windows in the church telling the history of the Guermantes family, and the Duchesse once seen sitting in her family booth on the balcony of the church, separated from the community, and the Guermantes walk impossible to complete because their castle was forbidden territory to the child. Now Gilberte points out to him that they can visit the castle by just continuing the Méséglise way for another quarter of an hour. All the enchantment had gone, he had reached the goal and gotten to know the Guermantes in all their niceties, vices, and narrowness, and Gilberte now was a member of this family by being married to Saint-Loup. The walks are not anymore sources of loving affection, rather of disillusions (Vol. 1:711): "But what struck me most forcibly was how little, during this stay, I re-lived my childhood years, how little I desired to see Combray, how narrow and ugly I thought the Vivonne." The perception of the surroundings is very much influenced by the affections one lives in. For the child the Méséglise way was so precious because he was in love with the little girl Gilberte he had once seen on his way at Tansonville, but could not meet her again since his parents did not approve of seeing her because of the doubtful reputation of her mother. Now he sees in Gilberte merely the daughter of Swann and Odette, and the wife of Saint-Loup. Loss of enchanting affection is something natural, not only in growing old, but also in the different phases of life (Vol. 3:714): "It is said, and this is what accounts for the gradual disappearance of certain nervous affections, that our nervous system grows old. This is true not merely about our permanent self, which continues throughout the whole duration of our life, but of all our successive selves, which after all, to a certain extent compose it."

When people loose the connection of sensory impressions to motor activity, they cannot orient themselves; they don't find their way; impressions then are not embedded into courses of action. When people loose the connections to the 'memory images', which contain a combination of previous perception and action, they cannot achieve a general conceptual characterization of sensory impressions that would be adequate to the situation (Bergson 1908:89).

Bergson discusses brain lesions and cognitive deficiencies of different kinds, among others, different kinds of reading problems: If the connection to the (pre-)motor activity is lost a patient cannot draw boundaries, not wholes, but merely isolated parts. He cannot recognize a whole object, but merely attends to some conspicuous parts (1908:94). – This, of course, reminds us on Oliver Sack's patient who took his wife for a hat. He just attended to the roundness, which is common to a hat, as well as to a face. – The boundaries of an object are detected by trying out fine movements in checking these against sensory input. Likewise the boundaries of a known object are recognized by those fine movements, which have been fixed in memory. Memory makes the sensory experience finer and guides the interaction of the body with the sensory impressions, in which a memorized routine is weighed as fitting or not fitting with the sensory impression, and in which other fitting routines are searched for in the case a routine is unfit. Recognizing an object is described as a series of tests with "memory images", general concepts, and motor routines. Bergson describes the interaction between body and object as circuits between memory and object, whereby in interaction circuits of sensory impressions with "memory images", i.e. general concepts and routines, modify the impressions by integrating aspects into the unity of an object (1908:98–103). In this way a perception is created.

Bergson (1908:107–108) elaborates this principle of circuit activity when dealing with the role of memory in language, especially its function for the recognition of spoken words by making connections between acoustic schemata and motor routines, i.e. articulation schemata. There are patients who are able to imitate spoken words exactly without being able to recognize the words. Here we have imitation using short time memory, without the long time (generalizing) memory for schemata and routines (1908:114–115). He also reports from psychiatric and psychological literature that memory for verbs, which have an essential connection to the brain's motor facilities, stays intact longest, while proper names are forgotten fast.

Bergson stresses the overall dynamics of understanding: understanding does not consist in a sequence of separate steps and representations. Rather it is a holistic activation in which expectations about the speaker, the language, the kind of ideas, the intonation play a role. There are no remembrances or images in separate nerve cells. Instead of assuming a collection of representations or images in our memory we rather should assume something like signs indicating the direction of a path (1908:126). In our present terminology introduced in the section above on Memory, these are indicators or indices, which have more or less strong connections to each other and to the sensory and motor areas of the brain, and to indicators of spatial and temporal relationships. The dynamics of perception and memory takes place in a unifying process (1908:128), whereby the memory activates the sensory regions, in mirror-symmetry to the impressions of the external object as activator of

the sensory regions (1908: 130–133). The affections of the body, which constitute consciousness, are produced by the contact of sensory activity caused from
out the memory, "the mind's ear", with sensory activity caused from out the
sense organs, "the outer ear", via stimulation caused by the object (1908: 133).
This metaphorical description is still a valid model of the dynamics of perception, action, and memory, as it is developed in *Consciousness Emerging*
(Bartsch 2002).

Memory itself is merely virtual, a disposition or capacity to remember; it
is, by itself not directed towards motor activity. That is only the case, when
memory gives rise to a remembrance, i.e. when it emerges in a materializa-
tion as an affection by melting together with an impression or concrete image.
Only when a memory disposition materializes into an image it can take part in
shaping the presence and being part of our activity. Pure memory is an unconscious, powerless state of our mind. Consciousness is imaging, remembering,
perceiving, and action (1908: 143). Bergson has difficulties in describing what
memory is because he cannot say clearly how the virtuality or the dispositional
character of the memory is materially real. For that he would need the connectionist neuro-cognitive model we have available today. He therefore talks, in
the traditional terminology of cognitive science, about an unconscious mind
as all the unconscious representations, which is what has the potential to become conscious, for example, what is outside of the perception of this room
and of which I know that it exists. Likewise I know that the past existed. The
matter, the world for us, is according to Bergson the whole set of all images,
the actual and the virtual ones (1908: 145). The assumed hidden mind together
with the conscious mind, and the world outside seem to be one and the same
thing. On the other hand he tries to understand the existence of the world
outside our consciousness as a hypostatization, i.e. assumed as an underlying
necessary order among the objects of our consciousness. There must be a chain
in the spatial and temporal memory and possible perception. Existence of an
object then means conceptualizing of sensory input in consciousness, i.e. in
perception, and embedding it within the order of space and time (1908: 148).
Existence, in this way, always is 'In-Existence', as Husserl (1939) has called it
in *Erfahrung und Urteil*, that is 'existence-in', namely being determined and
identified within the connectedness of a larger whole or horizon, finally the
universe, of which we cannot say anymore in a meaningful way that it exists or
doesn't exist, since existence is always existence within something larger.

Bergson paraphrases his philosophy of memory in many ways. A selection
of what he has to say illustrates this. He claims that, even though our perception is a matter of a moment, it nevertheless consists of an uncountable mass of

remembered elements, and therefore every perception is already remembering (1908:153). This accords well with the way Proust treats perception and understanding of objects, landscapes, towns, persons, and situations. Each episode and surrounding is painstakingly described in a representation that makes explicit its roots in the past experiences. The latter are revived in order to cast their light on the present in enhancing the common aspects.

The memory of the past is materialized in the whole sensory-motor system; it is the progressively expanding basis of experience. Bergson argues that the memory of the body, which is composed from the whole of the sensory-motor systems and which is organized by our habits and what we are used to, is the momentary memory at work in experiencing and understanding, the basis of which is the memory of the past (1908:156). This means that the whole of our faculties is memory. In each situation the requirements of action select from the memory what is useful, from the general memory the relevant conceptualization, and from the specific memory a relevant episode serving as a model for the present action. Because of this, remembrance at the first sight seems to be punctual, without connectedness. But in reflection, the contiguity relationships of the punctual remembrance can be elaborated making use of the episodic memory with its contiguity ordering. We thus understand the present by relating it to the past, and project from there expectations into the future. Memory can also be activated without being bound to present action, as in day-dreaming, or in near-death experiences (1908:157).

Bergson contrasts his position with nominalism on the one hand, and conceptualism, on the other: Nominalism does not assume general representations, general concepts, but rather merely extensions of similar objects, whereby only the symbol unites them, while Conceptualism takes the general representation, the concept, as starting point, which makes it possible to recognize similarity between objects. The first position faces the problem of how we can recognize similarity, and the second of how we can come into possession of a concept. Bergson's position is the one of Naturalism, namely that we establish an unconscious order-system according to similarities according to physical laws, with selections according to the needs of our motor system; habits and what we get used to is the basis for generality and general concepts. Following these basic capacities, our understanding finds and fixes similarity and general concepts and analyses them (1908:164). Bergson does not simply embrace the Psychology of association: the associations according to similarity and contiguity are not restrictive enough, because everything is similar to everything else in some way or other, and contiguity-relationships can always be established along some or other connected properties. Rather association has to be constrained by activity, action, movement and their requirements. What is useful provides the limitations for what is similar, and habits and motor routines provide the limitations for what is contiguous (1908: 171). The huge mass of potential remembrances of the past, which is comprised by memory, is made useful to us by becoming accessible following generalizations of different degrees, and following different systematizations (1908: 173). These ideas of Bergson's are very similar to the ones developed in the theory of concept formation and understanding of Bartsch (1998), which also takes the structural ordering relationships of similarity and contiguity as the basic principles for forming concepts as orderings on sets of data, whereby different perspectives, conditioned by the situational or linguistic context including goals, desires, actions, open up the modes of selection, for example different dimensions and similarity spaces. Among these selection devices are, of course, also those perspectives that are created by needs and restrictions due to the requirements of activities and actions in a situation.

3.   Individual and general concepts in Proust's novel

The most complex individual in *A la recherche du temps perdu* is Swann, son of a rich Jewish stock broker, who lived partly in Paris, partly on his country seat Tansonville, close to Combray. Different persons and circles in society entertain a different partial individual concept of Swann, depending on their experiences with Swann and their opinions on moral evaluation and values related to social strata. People try to accommodate their partial individual concept of Swann with other information about him by creating coherence between the different partial Swann-concepts such that their pre-established opinions are changed only minimally and the new information is interpreted and misinterpreted such that coherence is possible.

The person Swann, as the Narrator's great-aunt and grand-parents know him, is the son of his father, who was a middle class, well-of banker, a friend of the family, and a frequent house guest at Combray. No special talents are here accredited to Swann, and when young Marcel's family-members hear or read in *Figaro* that he takes part in receptions and festivities at the houses of famous politicians or fashionable dukes and princes, and in fashionable clubs of Paris, they either try to discard this information or try to fit it into their own concept of Swann by either interpreting it as attesting to a bad character of an up-shot, who mingles with those to whom he does not belong, or by lowering the so-called high society to the level of people who mix with morally doubtful actors, artists, and prostitutes. Swann had married the former prostitute Odette, who, as well as their common daughter, is not well-come for the Combray families to make acquaintance with. Swann is at least three different persons, the rich middle class country-man associating with his Combray friends, the former lover and then husband of Odette, the esteemed society-man in high-brow salons, who is known also as an art collector and writer of art critiques.

Proust writes about creating individual concepts (Vol. 1:20) that

> none of us can be said to constitute a material whole, which is identical for everyone..., our social personality is a creation of the thoughts of other people. Even the simple act which we describe as "seeing someone we know" is to some extent an intellectual process. We pack the physical outline of the person we see with all the notions we have already formed about him, and in the total picture of him, which we compose in our minds, those notions have already the principal place. In the end they come to fill out so completely the curve of his cheeks, to follow so exactly the line of his nose, they blend so harmoniously in the sound of his voice as if it were no more than a transparent envelope, that each time we see the face or hear the voice it is these notions which we recognize and to which we listen. And so, no doubt, from the Swann they had constructed for themselves my family left out, in their ignorance, a whole host of details of his life in the world of fashion, details which caused other people, when they met him, to see all the graces enthroned in his face and stopping at the line of his aquiline nose as at a natural frontier; but they had contrived also to put into his face divested of all glamour, vacant and roomy as an untenanted house, to plant in the depth of these undervalued eyes, a lingering residuum, vague but not unpleasing – half memory and half oblivion – of idle hours spent together after our weekly dinners, round the card table or in the garden, during our companionable country life. Our friends corporal envelope has been so well lined with this residuum, as well as various earlier memories of his parents, that their own special Swann had become to my family a complete and living creature; so that even now I have the feeling of leaving someone I know for another quite different person, when going back in memory, I pass from the Swann whom I knew later and more intimately to this early Swann – this early Swann in whom I can distinguish the charming mistakes of my youth, and in fact is less like his successor than he is like the other people I knew at that time, as though ones life where a picture gallery in which all the portraits of anyone period had a marred family likeness, a similar tonality – this early Swann abounding in leisure, fragrant with the scent of the great chestnut-tree, of baskets of raspberries and of a sprig of tarragon.

In this passage we see the creation of an individual concept, which is always partial, seen from different points of view, namely the individual seen from different points of view. However, the partial individual concept is projected into a complete individual by relating the different partial individual concepts to the same name and striving at coherence between the facets and situations that make up the individual's life-history. We see that the individual concept entertained by one subject, here the Narrator, is a rich collection of situations in which the individual has been met, and that these situations are called up by those aspects that were prominent for the remembering subject, here the scent of the chestnut-tree, the raspberries Swann brought for the family on his visits, and the smell of tarragon from his garden. Like the experience of scents also the sphere of the hours of leisure spent together form part of the individual concept of Swann, as it is created in the Narrator's childhood in Combray. Proust distinguishes the essence of an individual from the various individual concepts formed of it (Vol. 3: 1023):

> No doubt, life by placing each of these people on my path a number of times, had presented them to me in particular circumstances which, enclosing them finally on every side, had restricted the view which I had of them and so prevented me from discovering their essence. For between us and other people there exists a barrier of contingencies, just as in my hours of reading in the garden at Combray I had realized that in all perception there exists a barrier as the result of which there is never absolute contact between reality and our intelligence.

The situations in which the individual appears are wrapped in a veil of contingencies, which is lifted by the imagination of the Narrator, or the one who forms the individual concept. In his imagination he drives at what is typical of this individual's life, and also of this kind of individual in his natural and social setting. Imagination is the work of our understanding (Vol. 3: 998): "…pleasure was something I had never felt except when I was alone and the real differentiation of impressions takes place only in our imagination." Imagination depends on the workings of the memory; it has its roots in the generalizations and associations, which our brain forms on the impressions and excitations we get from the outside when interacting with our surroundings.

We furthermore see in the last quotation how the individual concepts of persons living at a certain time, in a certain area, in similar ways of life, or in similar situations, get lined up in a sequence, which forms the basis of a general concept of this kind of individuals in certain kinds of circumstances. The Swann of the Narrator's youth is experienced as being more similar to other people living in similar surroundings in the same period of time, than he is experienced as being similar to the Swann known later in life. The partial individual concept of Swann at a certain period of time contains a generalization with respect to other individuals in similar social and cultural positions, which the understanding author of the individual concept has encountered: When forming an individual concept, we compare the individual and his ways to others for similarities and differences, whereby both are stressed, the similarities under the relevant perspectives of social roles, and the differences typical for the respective individual. The general concept of a man of certain social standing at a certain time is formed across the many partial individual concepts as being time slices at a certain time, rather than across the whole individuals, i.e. across the whole individual life histories.

Not only the same social settings contribute to the similarity between different men encountered by the Narrator at the same period. Rather the state of the Narrator's mind and affections contribute an aspect of similarity to the different men at that period. To some extent the subject creates the object, as had also been pointed out by Bergson, where the object of perception and knowledge is created by a circuit interaction between the object and the perceiving and thinking subject. Also other persons, or rather individual concepts, are created in these interactions of impressions, originating from out the object, with the state of mind, the memory, the affection of the subject, as we have seen in the previous section.

A la recherche contains many encounters with Swann, also later in the Narrator's life and at different places and occasions in different social settings, up to his death. Hereby the real referent of an individual concept and it's rigidly referring name, of course, establish the physical and social contiguity between the different partial individual concepts by which these parts are part of a whole. However, the contiguity of the personal traits across time is difficult to establish, or even sometimes lacks when the occasions are very different, or a long period of time has elapsed. For the Narrator, Swann is several different persons in different settings, and especially in different periods of life, though they are all anchored in the Swann of Marcel's childhood, as he is remembered in *Time Regained*, via a path leading from meeting his daughter Gilberte, now the widow of the Guermantes' nephew Saint-Loup, and meeting their young daughter, now a girl of 16. In them, Swann's way, that is the Méséglise way, and the Guermantes way (representing the two types of society the Narrator lives in) have flown together. From there, at the end of the novel, the Narrator finds his starting point for writing down the entire novel, from the beginning in Combray, as the history of his life. He, like Swann, takes part in, but also distances himself, from the two societies, bound together in these life-histories, which establish the individual concepts of Marcel and of Swann.

By writing the novel, the Narrator investigates his own 'essence', as he calls his unconscious self, which makes him perceive and conceptualize the world as his world, by laying out within his life-history the lines that connect the episodes, individuals, objects, places, societies, and epochs in his understanding. Hereby he shows his unconscious process of concept formation and the resulting memory at work in ordering his experiences under the conditions of his individual sensitivity, tendencies, habits, attitudes and other perspectives of his personal interaction with the world around him. In this interaction of the personal pre-conditions with the world, episodes come into consciousness and are investigated in their inter-relatedness, in which these unconscious pre-conditions show themselves in the resulting episodes and in the structures between episodes. The unconscious hereby gets an extensional, outward representation in the whole ordered set of episodes. Thus it is exteriorized in episodic consciousness. In this way, the Narrator documents his attempt to probe into the unconscious and to investigate his own 'essence'.

Also Bloch, the friend of the young Narrator, appears to him as a different person from what he had been as a youth, when he meets him 25 years later. He now has more likeness with his father at the same age in features and behavior, which the Narrator clearly remembers, when seeing Bloch. The young Bloch is no more. There is the replica of his father in looks, habits, and social behavior, prototypical in several aspects for his (Semitic) race, as Proust remarks, like the Guermantes show the features and habits of the Guermantes clan, evident for centuries in the old portraits gallery.

> I had always considered each one of us to be a sort of multiple organism or polyp, not only at a given moment of time...but also similarly where the personality is concerned, and its duration through life, I had thought of this as a sequence of juxtaposed but distinct "I's", which would die one after the other or even come to life alternately, like those which at Combray took one another's place within me when evening approached. But I had seen also that these moral cells of which an individual is composed are more durable than the individual himself. I had seen the vices and the courage of the Guermantes recur in Saint-Loup, as also at different times in his life his own strange and ephemeral defects of character, and as in Swann his Semitism. And now I could observe the same phenomenon in Bloch.

The Narrator illustrates this by using an analogy to the sequence of the projections caused by the magic lantern of his childhood throughout his room in Combray (Vol. 3:973):

> ...so that just as, in listening to the conversation of Cottard and Brichot and
> so many others, I had felt that, through the influence of culture and fashion,
> a single undulation propagates identical mannerisms of speech and thought
> through a whole vast extent of space, it seemed to me now that throughout
> the whole duration of time great cataclysmic waves lift up from the depth of
> ages the same rages, the same sadness, the same heroism, the same obsessions,
> through one superimposed generation after another, and that each geological
> section cut through several individuals of the same series offers the repetition,
> as of shadows thrown upon a succession of screens, of a picture as unchanged –
> though often not so insignificant – as that of Bloch exchanging angry words
> with his father-in-law, M. Bloch the elder doing the same in the same fash-
> ion with M. Nissim Bernard, and many other pairs of disputants whom I had
> myself never known.

Individuals are seen as typical for their family origin and the history of their social group. When we identify and understand persons we take them as members
and products of their milieu, as shown in the individual concepts which are revealed in a cross-section through space, and also as the individual concepts
shown and compared in the succession of time. The individual concept comprises the general concepts that are typical under these horizontal and vertical
time slices in their historical, cultural, and social respects. There are synchronic
and diachronic similarities, which are the basis of general concepts, synchronic
ones, as well as diachronic ones, which generalize over historical concepts, for
example individual concepts. Taking the synchronic slices in diachronic order,
we construct historical concepts of groups, as are sorts, races, or clans and families of individuals. These historical general concepts express themselves in the
individuals of the respective groups.

Only the individual itself is able to see the contiguity and richness of his
own life-history by activating his memory, and thus only the Narrator himself can show how time is regained by constructing the history of his own life,
the individual concept of himself. Seen from the outside, an individual just is
a collection of fragments, partial individual concepts, whereby the identity is
established, often with difficulty, by a combination of some physical and social traits, such as the individual's name, and often by some or other personal
tic. Therefore the history of the Narrator must be the topic in an investigation
into the formation of a complete individual concept. Only the Narrator himself
can transcend the partiality in his consciousness, but only restricted to his own
perspective, and as far as his memory goes.

In the last part of the novel with the title *Time Regained*, the Narrator, after
about 15 years of absence, meets again the people of the old aristocratic and

bourgeois circles at a party given by the Prince and Princess de Guermantes. The two societies have come together, like the Guermantes and the Méséglise way in the surroundings of Combray, by several marriages of bourgeois money with aristocratic name. Marcel believes himself to be in a theatre where all the acquaintances of former times are in the disguise of old age that resists recognition. With respect to the Prince of Guermantes he writes (Vol. 3:960):

> So successful was his disguise that I recognized him only by a process of logical deduction, by referring from the mere resemblance of certain features the identity of the figure before me...Still greater was my surprise when a moment later I heard the name Duc de Chatellerault applied to a little elderly man with the silvery moustaches of an ambassador, in whom, thanks to a tiny fragment which still survived of the look that I remembered I was just able to recognize the youth whom I had once met at Mme de Villeparisis's tea-party. The first time that I thus succeeded in identifying somebody, by trying to dismiss from my mind the effects of his disguise and building up, through an effort of memory, the whole familiar face around those features which had remained unaltered, my first thought ought to have been ... to congratulate him for having made himself up with such wonderful skill...

And his old time enemy M. d'Argencourt he now sees with detestation (Vol. 3:961):

> He had turned into a contemptible old beggar-man, and the diplomat, whose solemn demeanor and starched rigidity where still present to my memory, acted his part of old dotard with such verisimilitude that his limbs were all of a tremble and the features of what had once been a haughty countenance were permanently relaxed in an expression of smiling idiocy. Disguise, carried to this extent, ceases to be a mere art, it becomes a total transformation of personality. And indeed, although certain details assured me that it was really Argencourt who presented this ludicrous and picturesque spectacle, I had to traverse an almost infinite number of successive states of a single face if I wished to rediscover that of the Argencourt whom I had known and who was now, though he had no other materials than his own body with which to effect the change, so different from himself.

On the observational level there is no unity of a coherent (complete) individual concept through time. But by imagination and interpolation we fill in periods of missing observation, whereby an individual concept can be constructed with a local, temporal, and causal coherence between stretches of time. I shall spare you the further dreadful details of the description of the old Argencourt and present here some of the Narrator's conclusions (p. 962) which continue with:

And this was not because of any survival of my old feeling of antipathy, for indeed he had so far become unlike himself that I had the illusion of being in the presence of a different person, as gentle, as kindly, as inoffensive as the other Argencourt had been hostile, overbearing, and dangerous. So far a different person that the sight of this hoary clown with his ludicrous grin, this snow-man looking like General Dourakine in his second childhood, made me think that it must be possible for human personality to undergo metamorphoses as total as those of certain insects.

The whole party becomes a puppet show in which Time gets exteriorized (p. 964):

One was obliged to study them at the same time with one's eyes and with ones memory. These were puppets bathed in the immaterial colors of the years, puppets which exteriorized Time which by Habit is made invisible and to become visible seeks bodies, which wherever it finds it seizes, to display its magic lantern upon them. As immaterial now as Golo (my explanation: a figure projected by the magic lantern) long ago on the door-handle of my room at Combray, the new, the unrecognizable Argencourt was here before me as the revelation of Time, which by his agency was rendered partially visible, for in the new elements which went to compose his face and his personality one could decipher a number which told one the years of age, one could recognize the hieroglyph of life – of life not as it appears to us, that is to say permanent, but as it really is: an atmosphere so swiftly changing that at the end of the day the proud nobleman is portrayed, in caricature, as a dealer in old clothes.

And about a lady he had known as a young girl he concludes after a thorough description (p. 965):

All these new features of the face implied new features also of the character; the thin, severe girl had turned into a vast and indulgent dowager. And no longer in a zoological sense, as with M. d'Argencourt, but in a social and moral sense one could say of her that she was a different person.

The Narrator, author of the individual concepts, constructs a more complete individual concept across time by interpolation (p. 965):

For all these reasons a party like this at which I found myself was something much more valuable than an image of the past: it offered me as it were all the successive images – which I had never seen – which separated the past from the present, better still it showed me the relationship that existed between the present and the past; it was like an old-fashioned peepshow, but a peepshow of the years, the vision not of a moment but of a person situated in the distorting perspective of Time.

In such a situation we experience the reality of time, and we regain Time, that is things lost, by remembering, and also by coherently imagining what we cannot remember, because we had not experienced the missing phases of a life-history.

The Narrator himself, in his own consciousness, does not realize that he also has grown old. His hair is still black. But it is more that the 15 years away from society, living the daily routine of the sanatorium with nothing new to happen, lets him experience the time elapsed as short. Mere habit and routine, repetition of events which we only perceive in their long established generality, without exciting and remarkable episodes that differentiate time in our memory, make us loose time. Afterwards, 15 years seem like a day, like it also happens when we grow old (cf. Draaisma 2001, *Why time goes faster when we get old*). Apparently, this phase in the history of the Narrator is not worth to be remembered, at least not in the context of a research into the society in which the Narrator places himself and the construction of his own individual concept. Those years in the sanatorium are not relevant, except as a large gap that makes it possible to realize the contrast between the earlier and the later state of the social world he lives in.

Marcel sees himself still as the young man of 15–20 years ago, when he asks the now aged Gilberte, the daughter of Swann, and the love of his childhood, whether he, a young man, would be the right company for her, when she invited him to go to dine in a restaurant. He only realizes his fault when everybody around bursts into laughter, and then he corrects his words into 'old man'. Marcel himself wants to get introduced to Gilberte's daughter, 16 years old, and in becoming friends with her he wanted to re-live his memories of the other young women he had loved in his youth. But he gets shocked when the girl answers that it might be interesting for a young person to make his acquaintance and hear about the experiences and the opinions of an old man. Realizing his own old age now teaches the Narrator that as an author of a novel he cannot capture and understand reality by describing time-slices of the geographical and social space and enhancing what is typical of such periods, but that he has to connect the periods by cutting through the length of time (Vol. 3:973–974):

> And now I began to understand what old age was – old age which perhaps of all the realities is the one of which we preserve for the longest in our life a purely abstract conception, looking at calendars, dating our letters seeing our friends marry and then in their turn the children of our friends, and yet, either from fear or from sloth, not understanding what all this means, until the day we behold an unknown silhouette, like that of M. d'Argencourt, which teaches us that we are living in a new world...

What we experience during a time-slice or phase in our life are situations that are aspectualized or conceptualized by the situational concepts and partial individual concepts formed in connecting previous impressions of situations and objects to other similar ones within the same time-slice. Proust here speaks of images we form of the things around us. They stand before the things, when we perceive and understand them. When we see things in the course of time we can form more complete individual concepts of them across time and then we reach to what he calls 'ideas' or 'essences', which are concepts of full historical entities, not only of individuals, but also of types of individuals, of families, of ethnic and social groups, and concepts of the typical properties, ways of life, and relationships within these and between these. He writes (Vol. 3: 974):

> For if names had lost most of their individuality for me, words on the other hand now began to reveal their full significance. The beauty of images is situated in front of things, that of ideas behind them, so that the first sort of beauty ceases to astonish us as soon as we have reached the things themselves, the second is something that we understand only when we have passed beyond them.

He concludes this section on experiencing old age with the insight that not only impressions, 'the beauty of images', which exemplify general concepts that are outside time, have to be the material of his novel, rather Time has to be included in showing the different ways in which living beings, but also social groups, and nations change and also keep constancy and coherence in change (Vol. 3: 974): "The cruel discovery which I had just made could not fail to be of service to me so far as the actual material of my book was concerned." The book is not to be just an impressionistic novel, rather also a historical one, about the history of typical fictional persons and societies.

In experiencing change, Time Lost has been regained under the guise of new features from where old features shine in a distorted form and episodes connected to these are re-called. Some individuals have changed mostly in physical appearance, others display a great change in moral character and thus have changed their personality, either by growth of moral experience or ability. Some show only little change. The Narrator plays through all kind of physical, personal, and social changes, which the now aged acquaintances of his younger years have undergone, many to the worse, some to the better. He also shows the workings of Time with respect to the social relationships between individuals and social groups. Like the individuals, society has changed, too. Former personal sins and merits were forgotten, individuals got accepted and others excluded from the society of the Faubourg Saint-Germain. Groups that had been strictly separated now got mixed.

A partial individual concept we have of a person or object does not stay constant. It changes while it is retained in our memory because it is repeatedly re-used not only in referring again to the same individual in other places, at other times, and thus growths in time, but also because it gets activated by encountering similar persons and objects, or similar surroundings with other people and objects, such that what is typical for them reflects on the original persons and objects. Proust describes this process in a poetical manner:

> How often had all these people re-appeared before me in the course of their lives, the diverse circumstances of which seemed to present the same individuals always, but in forms and for purposes that were shifting and varied! And the diversity of the points in my life through which, like so many interwoven threads, those of each of these personages had passed had in the end brought into conjunction even those that seemed the furthest apart from another, as though for the execution of infinitely varied patterns life possesses only a limited number of threads. ... And yet to-day all these different threads had been woven together to form the fabric, there of the married lives of Robert and Gilberte Saint-Loup, here of the young Cambremer couple, not to mention Morel and all the others whose conjunction had played a part in forming a set of circumstances of such a nature that the circumstances seemed to me to be the complete unity and each individual actor in them merely a constituent part of the whole. And by now my life had lasted so long that not infrequently, when it brought a person to my notice, I was able, by rummaging in quite different regions of my memory, to find another person, unlike though with the same identity, to add to and complete the first.   (Vol. 3: 1019–1020)

A partial individual concept formed in a certain situation is connected to re-membered partial individual concepts of the same individual, "the same identity", and thus a more complete historical concept of the individual is achieved. In this way the individual encountered in a certain situation is identified and thus recognized. Identification is one aspect of understanding. The general process of understanding a situation is here described as embedding it into a web of similarity and contiguity relationships, whereby also contiguity relationships within certain situational constellations are experienced as similar to other such relationships, and are seen in this way as typical. Memory makes understanding possible. The same holds for understanding paintings. Also they get embedded into a web of coherence (Vol. 3: 1020):

> Even to the Elstirs, which I saw hanging here in a position which was itself an indication of his glory, I was able to add very ancient memories of the Ver-

durins, the Cottards, my first conversation with the painter in the restaurant at Rivebelle, the tea-party in his studio at which I had been introduced to Albertine, and a host of other memories as well.

This is a very personal way of understanding something through integrating it into one's own life-history by relating it to individual and situational concepts one has acquired previously. The general method of understanding works of art and cultural manifestations, but even of natural objects and surroundings is of the same kind. Throughout the novel, various churches at different places in different natural and cultural surroundings, their architecture and their interiors, sculptures, and paintings are described by relating them to similar ones previously encountered by the Narrator, and by elaborating their social and cultural setting. Proust goes on with a metaphor characterizing the process of remembering (Vol. 3:1020):

> Thus a connoisseur of painting who is shown one wing of an altar-piece remembers in what church or in which museums or whose private collection the other fragments of the same work are dispersed and, in the same way as by studying the catalogues of sales and haunting the shops of antique-dealers he finds, in the end, some object which is a twin to one he already posses and makes a pair with it, he is able to reconstruct in his mind the predella and whole altar as they once were. And just like a bucket being hauled up by a winch swings first against one side of the descending rope and then against the other until it has touched it at every point, so there was scarcely a character, scarcely even a thing which had found a place in my life and had not turn and turn about played in it a whole series of different roles. If after an interval of several years I rediscovered in my memory a mere social acquaintance or even a physical object, I perceived that life all this while had been weaving round person or thing a tissue of diverse threads which ended by covering them with the beautiful and inimitable velvety patina of the years, just as in an old park a simple runnel of water comes with the passage of time to be enveloped in a sheath of emerald.

The Narrator, in his struggle to become the author of his envisaged great literary work, was aware of the fact that the strength of memory and the activity of remembering made possible an understanding which would create the structure of the whole novel, which was the conceptual structure of his life-history, the truth of his life, which does not depend on whether this or that event had really happened, this or that person, object, or place really existed, this or that thought had been really thought, but which was such that it was typical of a life of this type of person in these types of natural and social surroundings. He writes (Vol. 3:1102):

> But was not the re-creation by the memory of the impressions which had then
> to be deepened, illumined, transformed into equivalents of understanding,
> was not this process one of the conditions, almost the very essence of the work
> of art as I had just now in the library conceived it?

The equivalents of understanding are the concepts in the overall conceptual
structure we develop in understanding our world; they are the general concepts
of objects and situations, and they are the historical, especially the individual concepts of objects, places, people, families, societies, and nations. And all
these concepts have to be represented in partial extensions. In fact, they only
have existence in these extensions, that is, in acts of exemplifications ordered by
similarity and contiguity under certain perspectives. Proust's viewed his work
as the exteriorization of a life-time memory, which is in fact – by way of modeling the conceptual structures in concrete and detailed examples of situations
and courses of events, of objects, of places and persons – an explication and an
exteriorization of the development of the conceptual structure that makes up
the Narrator's mind along the history of his life.

In Dynamic Conceptual Semantics (Bartsch 1998), an individual is represented by an individual concept. Individual concepts are partial. They are
sequences of situations in which the individual played a role, and the complete
individual concept is a coherent integration of all partial individual concepts
in time. A general concept is represented by a similarity set of situations, and
likewise a routine or habit is represented by a similarity set of own actions.
The world of a subject is a network of situations, which are ordered and thus
perceived and understood by being integrated into the representations of individual concepts, general concepts and routines, keeping intact there stability
and coherence. Understanding as embedding the new into the old can also
change the concepts because adding new situations to previously formed concepts, that is to previously formed representative sets of examples, may enhance
or even add features as being experienced as common in the old and the new
examples. If the embedding is not possible while retaining stability of the internal similarity of a general concept, or the coherence within a historical concept,
the new situation is experienced as deviant, and can be the starting point for
forming a new concept together with some previous and further new situations, or it can be nevertheless be integrated into an old concept, whereby the
old concept gets destabilized and changed into a new, modified, concept.

Applying this exposition of concept formation and understanding to *A la
recherche*, understanding a situation or episode, as the Narrator presents it to
us, means that we integrate it into the contiguity orders of sets of situations

forming individual and other historical concepts, and that we integrate it into similarity sets of situations forming general concepts and routines, keeping intact the similarity within the set. It can also mean that we experience deviance and that we form a new concept or modify an old concept, in order to adjust our conceptual system to the new situation.

By being used repeatedly, that means by being involved unconsciously in understanding new situations, and by being used in remembering, triggered by a new situation, our concepts, and especially our individual concepts, undergo some change, which even can lead to error (Vol. 3: 1022): "... people – and in saying "people" I mean "what people are for us" – do not in our memory possess the invariability of a figure in a painting. Oblivion is at work within us, and according to its arbitrary operation they evolve. Sometimes it even happens that after a time we confuse one person with another." This oblivion, we want to add, is not just forgetting, but it is due to the permanent re-weaving of the conceptual ordering in our mind, whereby further generalizations and connections are established which order our impressions into new types by generalization, and into new coherent wholes by exploring contiguity relationships. In Proust's literary composition this principle of concept formation and understanding is consciously employed as a method.

4.   The method of the author

Proust's method of the literary construction of the individual concepts is not the same as the forming of individual concepts by the Narrator within the novel. We have seen above how the narrator, Marcel in the novel, forms his individual concepts of the persons around him. The author of the novel, on the other hand, collected aspects and situations of several real persons into one fictional character, and, of course enriched and combined them by imagination. The Narrator writes about the method of the author (Vol. 3: 1091):

> and yet in another way my work would resemble that of Francoise: in a book individual characters, whether human or of some other kind, are made up of numerous impressions derived from many girls, many churches, many sonatas and combined to form a single sonata, a single church, a single girl, so that I should be making my book in the same way that Francoise made that *boeuf a la mode* which M. de Norpois had found so delicious, just because she had enriched its jelly with so many carefully chosen pieces of meat.

In combining aspects of several objects of a kind into one literary individual concept the author tries to capture generality, which he takes to be the truth or essence of the object, its type. In the terminology of Rosch's (1973, 1978) prototype-theory he constructs a psychological prototype of a category of objects, with which the members of the category have more or less features in common, depending on how typical they are for the category. Seen as constructs of a historian, they can be understood as Max Weber's 'Ideal-Typen'. It is expressed like this in *Time regained* (Vol. 3:945):

> And more even than the painter, the writer, in order to achieve volume and substance, in order to attain generality and, so far as literature can, to reality, needs to have seen many churches in order to paint one church and for the portrayal of a single sentiment requires many individuals. ... And when inspiration is born again, when we are able to resume our work, the woman who was posing for us to illustrate the sentiment no longer has the power to make us feel it. We must continue to paint the sentiment from another model, and if this means infidelity towards the individual, from a literary point of view, thanks to the similarity of our feelings for the two women, which makes the work at the same time a recollection of our past loves and a prophecy of our new ones, there is no great harm in these substitutions. And this is one reason for the futility of those critical essays which try to guess who it is that an author is talking about. A work, even one that is directly autobiographical, is at the very least put together out of several intercalated episodes in the life of the author – earlier episodes which have inspired the work and later ones which resemble it just as much, the later loves being traced after the patterns of the earlier. ... These substitutions add then to our work something that is disinterested and more general and they convey also the austere lesson that it is not to individuals that we should attach ourselves, that is not individuals who really exist and are, in consequence, capable of being expressed, but ideas.

This strategy is not only born out in the life of the author, but also in the ways of life the Narrator pursues. He explores the sentiment of love and jealousy in his relationship with his grandmother, his mother, Gilberte, Albertine, and in the relationships between Saint-Loup and Rachel, Saint-Loup and Gilberte, Charlus and Morel, Saint-Loup and Morel, and in a few other homosexual or lesbian relationships. Proust-fans have traced the sources of his literary characters and scenes leading to many different persons and episodes that have played a role in his life (see the biographies by Painter 1983; Tadié 2001; and the photo-book by Adams 1984).

One real character can be a source for more than one fictional character, and the traits and actions of several real characters can merge into one fictional character. These relationships between historical persons and Proust's literary figures are documented in Painter's biography and in W. H. Adams (1984), a book illustrated richly with portrait photos by Paul Nadar. Swann was modeled mainly on Proust's friend Charles Haas, but he also shows traits and habits of Proust himself. The love of Swann for Odette and his jealousy is replayed in some ways in the Narrator's love for Albertine. And this has some origins in the authors attachment to his friends Reynaldo Hahn and Alfred Agostinelli. The individual concept representing the Duchess de Guermantes formed from characteristics of Mme Émile Straus, Comtesse Laure de Chevigné, and Comtesse Élisabeth Greffulhe. But Mme Émile Straus was also a model for Odette, the former cocotte, mistress and wife of Swann, like it was also Méry Laurent, Mme de Bernadaky, and Laure Hayman. Their daughter Gilberte was modeled on Jean Pouquet, Comtesse de Martel, and Marie de Bernadaky. Baron Charlus was mainly based on Comte Robert de Montesquiou and the Prince Boson de Sagan. Marcel's friend Saint-Loup was a composition from Lt. Comte Armand de Cholet, Duc Armand de Guiche, Marquis Boni de Castelane, and the Vicomte Robert d'Humiere. The main basis for the Narrator's girlfriend Albertine was the Narrator's young chauffeur Alfred Agostinelli. Mme Aubernon de Nerville and Madeleine Lemaire were a source for Mme Verdurin, who kept the best known bourgeois salon, and who later in life as a rich widow married the Prince de Guermantes and thus became the Princess de Guermantes, paralleled by Odette, who, after Swann's death, then being a rich widow had married the nobleman de Forcheville, and hereby made her daughter Gilberte, as Mlle de Forcheville, and also herself a member of the circle around the Guermantes. Now finally the Méséglise way, which was Swann's way, and the Guermantes way were closed into one circle, like they did when walking around the town of Combray, the town of the Narrator's youth. The real persons that are the models for one or more literary figures contribute situations from their life-history, as they were experienced by the author, and they contribute emotional ties and all kinds of personal relationships, looks, character traits, and aspects of behavior. The goal of construing literary figures in this way was to create individual concepts of persons that were, in their ways, typical for human relationships and properties within and between the respective social groups, their history, their economic status, and their cultural expressions.

5. Individual concepts of places and objects

Not just individual concepts of persons, but also individual concepts of objects, places like the town Combray and the seaside resort Balbec, and walks in the vicinity of Combray are built up in the course of the novel and are a matter of reflection. Tadié reports (2001:89):

> We come across Ostende in *Jean Santeuil*, in the characteristic form of memory, since Proust lived events twice (at least): his actual, day-to-day existence, and his resurrection through memory. It was not when he was at this Belgian beach but ten years later that he thought and wrote, "And very close by was Ostende where he had been at a child...He was aware of a curious sensation as he thought of such a different past linking him with the present, and that by following the grey shore of this immense grey sea...he would reach Ostende...which for him was a beach that was cut off from the rest of the world." And so it was that as he recalled 'the North Sea, the Baltic and Dieppe', Jean observed 'that only Nature' by making us feel what we once felt before, can lead us to some point in the fabulous world of our memories which has become the world of truth.

Why is the world of our memories the world of truth? This is so because within the order of memory the conceptual structures are established by means of which we understand our world. They are the generalizations, the laws, established by similarity (including analogy as similarity in relationships) and the historical entities established by contiguity relationships and also similarity, which gives rise to historical types as generalizations over historical entities.

Tadié notices (2001:90) furthermore:

> The stimulus of the sea stirred the young man, drawn by the waves, the wind and the storms... Fascination by the sea... This Beaudelairian theme was complemented by another, which recalled nocturnal anxiety, the absence of the mother: 'The sea has the charm of those things that do not fall silent at night, which, in our restless lives, grant us leave to sleep, a promise that all will not vanish, like a night light for small children who feel less lonely when it glows.' (from *Les plaisirs et les jours*) ... we see very old thoughts and anxieties finding their way into the most recent phrases, and Ostende as a precursor of Trouville.

The sea as a background provides a level of calmness and constancy, a feeling of being at home, on which other feelings and experiences can emerge and develop into episodes that characterize a way of life, social contacts, routines, visits and excursions into the country side, which are repeated and modified in the several stays of the Narrator at Balbec. Here, social bonds are formed that create and reach into the episodes taking place in Paris, which is the main location of his life.

Churches and cathedrals are objects and places to which the autor has devoted much attention. The steeple of the church Saint-Hilaire of Combray, the first sign when approaching town, sometimes seems unreal and changing in memory like the scenes projected by the magic lantern in Marcel's Combray bed-room. The steeple is described repeatedly from different points of view, seen from the market square, seen when approaching from far away, looking at it from all sides and perspectives (p. 52, 68, 71, 72), comparing it to other church-steeples. The observer in his changing position, when traveling across the hilly countryside on a winding road, is taken as a fixed point such that the twin steeples of Martinville are changing in lines, positions, and illumination, and thus seem to perform a slow dancing movement, which is felt like a pretty phrase in words or in a piece of music. This deeply felt analogy, also with the moving reflections of the magic lantern, provides a pleasure in perceiving their seeming mobility (p. 196, 197). We see here and also in the elaborate descriptions of the interior of Saint-Hilaire (p. 64) as well as of other churches and cathedrals throughout the novel that the described objects get enlivened with movements, affection and spirit from out the movements, and associated with further affections, images, and thoughts of the observer. Thus the objects and places are constituted in our experience within the interaction circuit Bergson describes between our body and the object, between the body's movements, routines, memory, and the sensory impressions caused by the external object.

Proust had developed his manner of describing cathedrals when he translated Ruskin's works. Tadié (2001:345) gives us an account of what art is according to Ruskin, whose poetic descriptions of the architecture of cathedrals (*The Bible of Amiens, The Seven Lamps of Architecture, The Vale d'Arno, Praeterita*) Proust translated with the help of Marie Nordlinger:

> The artist stands between nature and ourselves. He is its interpreter, its celebrant and its memorialist. He immortalizes that which does not last, he discovers unfathomable laws, the mysteries from on high; he is the giver of joy. Like Emerson, John Ruskin observed that the artist discovers Beauty in the ephemeral leaf on a tree, in the tiniest pebble, 'the very simplest of objects, those that are most banal. Those most beloved sights that you see every summer evening along thousands of footpaths, the streams of water on the hillsides... of our old, familiar countryside'.

The objects, as they are experienced, are in this way a combination originating from their own primary properties and the way of perception and understanding projected as similarity and contiguity orderings, that is as categorization and positioning, onto the external object from out the experiencer. His perception is informed by his movements, his affections, and his memory, which has been built up by previous experiences of objects and scenes similar to the experienced object, perceived under the governing and changing perspectives. The perspectives, in the example of the twin steeples, are provided by the local and temporal relationships of these objects with the movements of the observer and other contiguity relationships in the situational contexts of the previously experienced similar objects, together with the habits in which the perceiver deals with his surroundings.

The Narrator has the habit of taking time for a free interplay of his moving around, perceiving, feeling, and his thinking with the objects and scenes he encounters. All his writing is an enactment reporting of this elaborate process of interaction between the Self and the world. The result is Marcel's world, the world created in this interaction. It is all part of the Narrator's consciousness, and it is not at all a kaleidoscopic stream of consciousness, rather a well structured and informed world, with elevated orientation points, persons and places, and with roads repeatedly followed through it. These are, for example, the Méséglise Way leading along and through Swann's property, and the Guermantes Way leading to the unapproachable castle of the Guermantes, two walks in opposite directions through the surroundings of Combray, which finally meet each other, and together form a circle around Combray. The Méséglise way is and symbolizes Swann's way, comprising the families of the Narrator, Bloch, Albertine, Odette, Gilberte, and the meetings with artists, writers, politicians, professors, and well-known physicians in the saloon of Mme Verdurin. Besides Swann, the Baron Charlus, a member of the Guermantes family, is a traveler between the worlds symbolized by these two walks. The two ways provide a structure of two elevated courses of events throughout the life-history of the Narrator, which meet in several manners during the adult life of the Narrator: by Swann's position within the aristocratic society, later paralleled by the Narrator's own position, by the marriages of Mme Verdurin, Odette, and Gilberte into these circles, and by Gilberte's and Saint-Loup's daughter, who later blends again by marriage with the world of artists and writers. This daughter is the embodiment of the union between different societies. The paths symbolize two kinds of social surroundings in his life, on the one side the social contacts with the people of the Méséglise Way, Swann and his family and other members of the higher or economically successful middle class, such as Marcel's friend Bloch and Madame Verdurin and her circle, and on the other side his life with the people of the Guermantes Way, the nobility of the time, princesses, dukes, duchesses, and comtes, like the Prince and Princess, and the Duke and Duchess of Guermantes, Baron Charlus, Saint Loup, and others. The two walks, described in their natural beauty, attractions, and enchantments for the child, provide an unconscious ground for experiencing the details concerning the two societies in which the Narrator lives; both, in nature and in society, the ways are "paths of exaltations of the mind", "two ways of life and of different experiences and longings, memories of locations and their attributes" (Vol. 1: 200–201).

The locations on the walks serve as orientation points in life, of "knowing and realizing of where one is." Life, the whole of episodic consciousness is ordered in paths of locations, objects, people, and episodes there taking place. People, places, episodes are related to each other by being similar to previous ones in one or other important respect, and by being connected in contiguity along paths of courses of situations and events. When later the two paths meet, they lose their mysteries for the Narrator and become something of the ordinary. Their contrast made them both interesting. When they had collapsed into each other, they became boring, just more of the same. That most of the experiences become just more of the same is the characteristics of growing older. It is therefore the possibility of re-living the ways of experiencing by the child and the youth he had been, which the elderly Narrator is after, but which can not be initiated voluntarily, it can only be given by accident, through a feeling, a bodily movement, a sudden impression, a sensation and emotion, which carries a previous episode in the way it had been experienced then, in a younger conceptual system, into the present, where it is strange, but still feels real. These remembered episodes are the elevated islands from where on and around which the Narrator revives, along the contiguities and similarities between episodes, individuals and places, his life as a child and as a younger man. Whether this really is possible, or just a dream or wish of the Narrator is much in question. In order to achieve this re-living of his youth, the child or young man must still be in him. How can that be if a conceptual system changes in the course of life and remembering is re-constructing, rather than tearing like a magician ready-made rabbits out of his hat?

The answer can only be found in the specific role of sensations, emotions, bodily feelings and the indices of the episodic memory, which together might select by activated connections conceptual indicators for re-constructing the episode not within their full adult connectivity to other conceptual indicators. They rather select or enlighten parts of the connectionist network of those constituting conceptual indicators that are not enhanced so much in the everyday adult life and are not overruled by the normal habitually activated connections of our concept indicators. In these special kinds of involuntary remembrances, the connections and herewith the interaction circuits with the emotional, sensory and motor parts of the brain might be stronger activated at the cost of the everyday connections between indicators of standard ontological and evaluative concepts. The intensity of the sensorial experience may momentarily take up so much physiological energy that the normal categorizations of the adult conceptual system are not activated enough to overrule the remembrance due to old connections established via these sensations with the vivid experiences of the youth of former times.

6.   The Past in the Present: Time Regained and timeless order

An example of similarity between episodes are those with the "*petites madeleines*", the cookies offered to Marcel at tea by his mother, soaking a piece in the tea on a tea-spoon (Vol. 1:48). This kind of scene is remembered also as part of the Sunday morning routine of visiting aunt Leonie in her bedroom, where she used to stay permanently. The madeleine cookie is dipped into blossom tea by aunt Leonie (p. 56). The remembrance of this scene later in life is caused via some material object, the cookie, contiguous with the remembered surrounding and episode. It further connects with the remembrance of the house, the square, the streets of Combray, the whole surrounding countryside, Swann's park, the Vivonne with its water lilies (p. 50). The important aspect of the original episode with his mother was the sensation of love felt when he tasted the soaked piece of madeleine. When later in life he had again tea and madeleines with his mother, he remembered the old scenes and what he had felt then. Not by the visual impression of the cookies or the tea, but by their taste and smell the whole sensations of the old scenes came back; he re-experienced the feeling of love and the happiness he had felt in the Sunday morning routines in Combray (p. 50–51), and herewith his whole Combray life was re-awakened in him.

In our model of memory, what happened here is that from a specific sensorial experience of taste and smell, via the activation of the neuronal indicators of similar sensations of the past, a whole network of conceptual indicators, and specific episodic indices of the memory is activated via the connections strengthened in experiencing the previous episode. From there activation hits the sensorial and motor fields and in this, by the activity of the interaction circuits between sensorial, motor, and conceptual and specific memory maps, the old scenes and episodes are experienced again as remembrances. Here Proust describes the act of remembering as a searching in memory (p. 49), which views memory still within the traditional model as a large file or library, while in fact it rather is an act of re-creating the remembrance in consciousness. At other places he rightly points out that the memory re-creates the remembered episodes, which gives room for constructions of remembrances, which are not fully identical with the previous episodes; rather in one remembrance several similar episodes can be blended together or aspects are added that in general can be found in an episode of this kind and therefore are expected, or these aspects can replace aspects of the previous episode.

Though a remembrance is constructed in an unconscious process, the result of the process appears to us in consciousness as a whole ready-made situation or episode. We are not aware of construing the episode, rather we have the whole before us in consciously experiencing the remembrance and we can attend to its parts and its relationships to other episodes. Each time such a remembrance gets unfolded by seeing in its similarity to other episodes, the Narrator reports experiencing an aesthetic or intellectual pleasure.

Another example is the remembrance caused by tripping against the uneven paving-stones in the courtyard of the mansion of the Prince de Guermantes, on arriving there in the evening of a grand party. A motor sensation reminds the Narrator of his tripping on uneven paving-stones in the Baptistery of St. Mark in Venice, and he re-lives much that was connected with that motor sensation. Here is the scene (Vol. 3: 898):

> Revolving the gloomy thoughts which I have recorded, I entered the court-yard of the Guermantes mansion and in my absentminded state I had failed to see a car which was coming towards me; the chauffeur gave a shout and I had just time to step out of the way, but as I moved sharply backwards I tripped against the uneven paving-stones in front of the coach house. And at the moment, when recovering my balance, I put my foot on a stone which was slightly lower than its neighbor, all my discouragement vanished and in its place was the same happiness which at various epochs of my life had been given to me by the sight of trees which I had thought that I recognized in the course of a drive near Balbec, by the sight of the twin steeples of Martinville, by the flavour of the madeleine dipped in tea, and by all those other sensations of which I have spoken and of which the last works of Vinteuil had seemed to me to combine the quintessential character. Just as, at the moment when I tasted the madeleine, all anxiety about the future, all intellectual doubts had disappeared, so now those that a few seconds ago had assailed me on the subject of the reality of my literary gifts, the reality even of literature, were removed as if by magic.

What now is common to all these episodes? His answer is the following:

> The emotion was the same; the difference purely material, lay in the images invoked, a profound azure intoxicated my eyes, impressions of coolness, of dazzling light, swirled round me and in my desire to seize them – as afraid to move as I had been on the earlier occasion when I had continued to savour the taste of the madeleine while I tried to draw into my consciousness whatever it was that it recalled to me – I continued, ignoring the evident amusement of the great crowd of chauffeurs, to stagger as I had staggered a few seconds ago, with one foot on the higher paving-stone and the other on the lower. Every time that I merely repeated this physical movement, I achieved nothing; but if I succeeded, forgetting the Guermantes party, in recapturing what I had felt when I first placed my feet on the ground in this way, again the dazzling and indistinct vision fluttered near me, as if to say: 'Seize me as I pass if you can, and try to solve the riddle of happiness which I set you.' And almost at once I recognised the vision: it was Venice, of which my efforts to describe it and the supposed snapshots taken by my memory had never told me anything, but which the sensation which I had once experienced as I stood upon two uneven stones in the baptistery of St. Mark's had, recurring a moment ago, restored to me complete with all the other sensations linked on that day to that particular sensation, all of which had been waiting in their place – from which with imperious suddenness a chance happening had caused them to emerge – in the series of forgotten days. In the same way the taste of the little madeleine had recalled Combray to me. But why had the images of Combray and of Venice, at these two different moments, given me a joy which was like a certainty and which sufficed, without another proof, to make death a matter of indifference to me?

Likewise the stiffness of a napkin brought back to him Balbec (p. 901)

> ...for the napkin which I used to wipe my mouth had precisely the same degree of stiffness and starchedness as the towel with which I had found it so awkward to dry my face as I stood in front of the window on the first day of my arrival at Balbec, and this napkin now, in the library of the Prince de Guermantes's house, unfolded for me ...the plumage of the ocean green and blue like the tail of a peacock.

Similar effects had the little phrase by Vinteuil for Swann, and then later for the Narrator, whose life partly was analogous to the life of Swann. In generalizing over episodes in linguistically guided concept formation and understanding, these little things like smells, tastes, movements, haptic sensations, little melodies which had no logical relationship with the main action, object, or participating persons of the episode did not become part of the general, and especially the semantic memory. Rather they had been connected to the specific memory and later the episode could be re-constructed from there (Vol. 3: 902–903):

> the slightest word that we have said, the most insignificant action we have performed at any one epoch of our life was surrounded by, and coloured by the reflection of, things which logically had no connection with it and which later have been separated from it by our intellect which could make nothing of them for its own rational purposes, things however, in the midst of which – ... – the simplest act or gesture remains immured as within a thousand sealed vessels, each one of them filled with things of a colour, a scent, a temperature that are absolutely different from one another, vessels, moreover, which being disposed over the whole range of years ... are situated in the most various moral attitudes and give us the sensation of extraordinarily diverse atmospheres.

What has been said here is that in the child's beginnings of concept formation and understanding also these sensorial aspects may be part of the formed experiential concepts as generalizations over these episodes, and they are certainly part of the specific episodes remembered. These sensorial aspects themselves are generalized within the sensory and motor systems; they are exemplifications of sensorial, emotional, proprioceptional and movement concepts. But in further linguistic use of the expressions describing this kind of episodes, the general concept expressed gets restricted to those aspects that are part of the normal inter-subjective use of the expressions describing the episodes. In the early years concept formation and understanding is based on a smaller set of experienced situations and also runs along more context specific aspects, including very personal impressions and expectations, than concept formation that later becomes important in the normal contexts of life, being rational, goal directed actions and normal expectations, often expressed linguistically.

Note that in repeating, on purpose, the movement of the foot when tripping on the uneven paving stones, and also the going back to Combray and Tansonville later in life for a visit of Gilberte, then the wife of Saint Loupe, and there trying to remember the old walks as a child at Combray by taking the same paths, does not call up in the Narrator the same feelings of emotional and sensorial richness that came about by an involuntary experience of the movement, of the haptic sensation, of the flavor, or the smell. A rational reconstruction of the scene by employing the normal, linguistically structured, situational concepts of episodes of this kind does not happen in the free space of consciousness that is needed for a full aesthetic experience and that is opened up by the unexpected movement, haptic sensation, taste or smell, or visual experience. The space in which the aesthetic experience of a situation takes place is free from current purposes and further goals, which as contexts would restrict the conceptualization, or aspectualization, of the situation by selecting concepts appropriate to these contexts. When no attention is given to the normal aspects of the present episode or situation, the aspects of the remembered episode can now be re-lived and also be described by the suitable linguistic expressions, which are now associated with expressions of those concepts that were connected in contiguity or similarity to the aspects of the previously experienced episode. These associated conceptualizations of the previous episode can come up and can provide for quite a different take-up of the present situation in other, for this situation not normalized aspects. The current situation can be blended with the remembered one, but it can also be seen in its contrast with the remembered situation, the contrast of what is different seen on the background of that what they have in common. Such a contrast can be an eye-opener, which implies an evaluation of both situations, taking into account their differences. This then can imply that one deals with the present situation differently than one would normally do.

Like in normal concept formation and understanding, the very special aspects that form part of the conceptualization of the remembered situation are also results of generalizing over several experienced episodes, but they are especially collections of personal experiences that had not yet been repressed by the selection of those aspects which fit into the normal contexts of common purposes and goals. The present experience fits to the previous one merely by repeating one very special accidental aspect. There is no consciously taken perspective under which this aspect had become part of the present experience. It just sprung up incidentally, without being expected. Instead of employing one or more of the standard perspectives, pre-installed for understanding a situation (What kind of object? What kind of texture / what kind of form? What color? What kind of movement? What face? What action?), which normally guide the selection of certain aspects of the situation, there is, with respect to the sudden sensation, no selection of further aspects pre-determined, rather there is the openness of non-selection by standard measures. In this way there is an open space for experience in which associated aspects provided by memory seem to show up freely. There must be some disposition towards pre-activation of certain attention spaces or conceptual sub-systems in the receptive individual that help the aspects come up strongly enough to be experienced. In the case of the Narrator, it must be so that sensory impressions and proprioceptional feelings must have been strongly connected to episodic indices and indicators of situational concepts in previous experiences. However, with respect to the remembered episodes, the Narrator's attention-space is not restricted by perspectives that are pre-determined by common purposes, such that only aspects pertaining to these purposes would be experienced. Rather a seemingly free play of perspectives opening up the possibility of different kinds of experiences of a situation is provided by spaces of conceptual indicators activated via episodic indices that are also strongly connected to certain sensorial and proprioceptional experiences. Possibly a narrowing, broadening, changing of such activated networks in a rhythmic manner can result in the experience of weaving aspects into a whole of an overall aesthetic experience (like "the tune of the little melody of Vinteuil"), which gives joy to the Narrator, and generally to the experiencing individual, and finally to the reader of the episodes which the author tries to present.

It is not the general memory, namely indicators of general situational concepts, that is the main mediator for an aesthetically relevant remembrance. Rather it is the episodic memory, which mediates between some little specific detail of an episode and the resulting remembrance. The episodic memory, invoked by some very specific current sensation, lets us remember and makes it possible for the Narrator to get to grips with, and to tell, his life-history in the fashion of a great writer (p. 903):

> Yes: if, owing to the work of oblivion, the returning memory can throw no bridge, form no connecting link between itself and the present minute, if it remains in the context of its own place and date, if it keeps its distance, its isolation in the hollow of a valley or upon the highest peak of a mountain summit, for this very reason it causes us suddenly to breathe a new air, an air which is new because we have breathed it in the past, that purer air which the poets have vainly tried to situate in the paradise and which could induce so profound a sensation of renewal only if it had been breathed before, since the true paradises are the paradises we have lost.

Only what is not anymore part of the type of the situation, namely of the general situational concept, indicated in the general memory and employed currently, can be experienced as new, although it had been experienced once. It is a renewed experience of an old episode, which is linked to the present episode by this common aspect, though the present context of this common aspect is totally different from the old one. And in the present context this aspect is not selected or enhanced as being part of the situational concept characterizing the present situation. These contexts even contrast with each other in such a way that the present context has to be cancelled for a moment in order for the old episode to re-appear in remembrance.

There are great differences between the episodes situated in different times and being connected with each other by a common sensation. The Narrator expresses this as the fact that the different episodes are differently located in the dimensions in which they have to be characterized. Although they have aspects in common they appear in a different light because of the different contexts and different personal experiential backgrounds, which enhance quite different aspects.

> And I observed in passing that for the work of art which I now, though I had not yet reached a conscious resolution, felt myself ready to undertake, this distinctness of different events would entail very considerable difficulties. For I should have to execute the successive parts of my work in a succession of different materials; what would be suitable for mornings beside the sea or afternoons in Venice would be quite wrong if I want to depict those evenings at Rivebelle when, in the dining-room that opened on to the garden, the heat began to resolve into fragments and sink back into the ground, while a sunset glimmer still illuminated the roses on the walls of the restaurant and the last water-colours of the day were still visible in the sky – this would be a new and distinct material, of a transparency and a sonority that were special, compact, cool after warmth, rose-pink.   (Vol. 3:903–904)

The episodes are painted in episodic memory, so to speak, in a different atmosphere, of morning, high noon, evenings, or nights. The atmosphere, the different contexts and different personal backgrounds of experience, is what connects them into sets of remembrances that reflect in their differences on each other. The atmospheres might be characterized by general experiential concepts that are kinds of emotions and sensations for which we have no ready-made linguistic indicator, because they are not topics of everyday talk. These aesthetic types or concepts characterized by such "atmospheric" aspects are other generalizations than everyday concepts. They get addressed via a sensorial, motor, or emotional present experience that also had been part of the previous, now remembered episode. The aesthetic types, for example the little melody by Vinteuil, provide for a rich network of scenes that are described in the novel as interrelated by these types. The lines of aesthetic presentation are seen as analogous to the lines in Vinteuil's melodies and in Bergotte's phrases. These aesthetic lines and phrases, the recurring theme's, for example of love, jealousy, and desertedness, in modifications are what re-occurs in the course of the novel. They define and bind together the essential scenes and episodes. Aesthetic memory does not work in temporal sequences, rather feelings and ways of being situated in "atmospheric" contexts hold them together in the remembrance of the Narrator. Though they are bound together by what they have in common, their essential differences are that what deserves attention. These are differences that are due to the change of the experiential and in consequence conceptual background in which the situations had been embedded in the different periods of life. The aesthetic memory is part of the episodic memory, as far as it is ordered through aesthetically relevant aspects.

When we go back to Vol. 2:412, we find the experience of the evenings in Rivebelle and their contrast with evenings at Doncieres and an evening in Combray:

> If as I came downstairs I re-lived those evenings at Doncieres, suddenly, when we reached the street, the almost total darkness, in which the fog seemed to have extinguished the lamps, which one could make out, glimmering very faintly, only when close at hand, took me back to a dimly remembered arrival by night at Combray, when the streets there were still lighted only at distant intervals and one groped one's way through a moist, warm, hallowed crib-like darkness in which there flickered here and there a dim light that shone no brighter than a candle. Between that year – to which in any case I could describe no precise date – of my Combray life and the evenings at Rivebelle which had, an hour earlier, been reflected above my drawn curtains, what a world of differences! I felt on perceiving them an enthusiasm which might have borne fruit had I remained alone and would thus have saved me the detour of many wasted years through which I was yet to pass before the invisible vocation of which this book is the history declared itself. Had the revelation come to me that evening, the carriage in which I sat would have deserved to rank as more memorable for me than Dr Percipied's, on the box seat of which I had composed that little sketch – which, as it happened, I had recently unearthed, altered and sent in vain to the *Figaro* – of the spires of Martinville. Is it because we re-live our past years not in their continuous sequence, day by day, but in a memory focused upon the coolness or sunshine of some morning or some afternoon suffused with the shade of some isolated and enclosed setting, immovable, arrested, lost, remote from all the rest, and thus the changes gradually wrought not only in the world outside but in our dreams and our evolving character (changes which have imperceptibly carried us through life from one time to another, wholly different) are eliminated, that, if we re-live another memory taken from a different year, we find between the two, thanks to lacunae, to vast stretches of oblivion, as it were the gulf of a difference in altitude or the incompatibility of two divergent qualities of breathed atmosphere and surrounding colouration? But between the memories that had now come to me in turn of Combray, of Doncieres and of Rivebelle, I was conscious at that moment of much more than a distance in time, of the distance that there would be between two separate universes whose substance was not the same. If I had sought to reproduce in a piece of writing the material in which my most

> insignificant memories of Rivebelle appeared to me to be carved, I should
> have had to vein with pink, to render at once translucent, compact, cool and
> resonant, a substance hitherto analogous to the sombre, rugged sandstone of
> Combra.   (Vol. 2:413)

In appearing, the remembrances are thus not steered by the order of time, but
they are triggered and steered by present or called-up sensations and bodily
feelings that are identical with sensations in previous episodes. By such identical sensory aspects the remembrance is rooted in the present and hereby
appears real. Still it is different from what is the present episode, because the
remembered episode carries with it from the past the context of experiencing it then, the special atmosphere, the other, different sensations and feelings.
Thus the past is regained in the present, but not in the same 'substance' as
the surrounding present experiences, rather its 'substance' or 'material' is of
the old kind, it feels differently, namely as the old reality, which now again
has become real because it has found roots in those identical sensations of
the present episodes by which it is triggered. This is Time Regained, in contrast with Time Present and Time Lost. It has to be distinguished from simple
blending between old and new episodes in which unconsciously formerly experienced aspects of the old situations are inserted into a newly experienced
situation. Since blending is an unconscious process we do not experience it as
such and thus are not aware of the cognitive operation that takes place here.
But in Proust's remembrances we consciously experience the present episode,
the identical sensations that trigger the past episode, and the past episode itself,
whereby the past becomes presently real, but not as the present reality, rather as
another reality, another world. Here the whole cognitive operation in its conscious constituent parts, in unearthing another reality, a hidden treasure, forms
the aesthetic experience, which Proust describes as feeling a happiness, a great
satisfaction. This reminds us of Kant's explanation of the feeling of aesthetic
pleasure, namely as experiencing ones own cognitive activity, the constituents
and the whole of one's own cognitive operations currently employed in constituting the resulting (aesthetic) object in an act of aesthetic arousal. However,
Kant did not pay any attention to the relationship between Past and Present.
For Proust, this feeling of Time Regained includes an experience of timelessness, of a kind of immortality of the experiencing self which, however it has
changed in the course of his life, has recovered his past in the present, and
will carry it into the future. Proust describes the aesthetic experience as a special cognitive operation involving the partial identity between present and past
episodes, and he explains the experience of the reality of the past by the roots it

has in the present. The experience does not involve a temporal relationship between the past and the present episode. Both seem equally present, presenting themselves alternately within their different worlds. The relationship between both is not a temporal one, but one of conceptual identity, mainly of types of emotions and sensations. Proust investigates the aesthetic experience in the following way (Vol. 3:904–908):

> Over all these thoughts I skimmed rapidly, for another inquiry demanded my attention more imperiously, the inquiry which on previous occasions I had postponed, into the cause of this felicity which I had just experienced, into the character of the certitude with which it imposed itself. And this cause I began to divine as I compared these diverse happy impressions, diverse yet with this in common, that I experienced them in the present moment and at the same time in the context of a distant moment, so that the past was made to encroach upon the present and I was made to doubt whether I was in the one or in the other. The truth surely was that the being within me, which had enjoyed these impressions, had enjoyed them because they had in them something that was common to a day long past and to the present, because in some way they were extra-temporal, and this being made its appearance only when, through one of these identifications of the present with the past, it was likely to find itself in the one and only medium in which it could exist and enjoy the essence of things, that is to say: outside time. This explains why it was that my anxiety on the subject of my death had ceased at the moment when I had unconsciously recognized the taste of the little madeleine, since the being which at the moment I had been was an extra-temporal being and therefore unalarmed by the vicissitudes of the future. This being had only come to me, only manifested itself outside of activity and immediate enjoyment, on those rare occasions when the miracle of an analogy had made me escape the present. And only this being had the power to perform that task which had always defeated the efforts of my memory and my intellect, the power to make me rediscover days that were long past, the Time that was Lost.   (Vol. 3:904)

These aesthetic moments of experiencing timelessness in Time Regained contrast with what is to follow in the latter part of this chapter, where, when taking part in a social gathering in the house of the Prince de Guermantes, the Narrator is confronted with all the acquaintances of his former years, which have aged over the last 15 years. This process of aging is described drastically by showing how the features of previously young persons still blend into those of the presently old person, often in a distorted way (see Section 2.2). The Past shows itself in the Present, but not as Time Regained. Rather, by contrasting what little is still preserved in a person with what is lost and is replaced by features of old age, the Narrator experiences Time Lost.

7. The aesthetic experience

The aesthetic experience is the basis for the Narrator to be able to write the novel. It constitutes his capacity of being a writer, for now he is able to see and describe the episodes of his life in the connectivity provided by the identity of the essential sensorial and emotional aspects of his experience. The course of time is not the only, and not the essential order between the episodes in this novel. For reaching this point, the Narrator had gone a long way of freeing himself for some 15 years from the everyday social encounters in a long period of absence spent in a sanatorium, where his asthma was treated. Disengagement, for some time, is a prerequisite of becoming engaged in life again, now in a different way, in which the change, the progress of Time, but also time-lessness of essential aspects can be experienced. New for the Narrator is the ability of transcending Time, eliminating change for a while and even, by this, having for a moment a feeling of timelessness, being without the fear of death, although in the reality of present events, the social gathering at the Prince de Guermantes, he repeatedly is aware of Time Lost in the course of life towards old age and death, when observing the other guests. When his memory creates a new world which is also the old, seemingly lost world of his youth, the aesthetic enjoyment of these cognitive abilities of memory is comprised by the phrase "the life of the mind and its joys", as we find it in what follows (Vol. 3:904):

> And perhaps, if just now I had been disposed to think Bergotte wrong when he spoke of the life of the mind and its joys, it was because what I thought of at that moment as "the life of the mind" was a species of logical reasoning which had no connection with it or with what existed in me at this moment – an error like the one which had made me find society and life itself tedious because I judged them on the evidence of untrue recollections, whereas now, now that three times in succession there had been reborn within me a veritable moment of the past, my appetite for life was immense.

What is common to the present remembrance, which for a moment seems real, and the past event which is remembered is what, in a timeless fashion, is part of the Narrator himself, namely of the background of his experiences and the conceptual structures or orderings formed on them, which make up the life-history, the individual concept of the Narrator himself. In other words, such a remembered episode, aspectualized (characterized, conceptualized) and thus understood by being embedded within the similarity and contiguity orderings established on the experiences forming the history of the experiencing subject, is part of his essence. The essence of the human being is his/her memory, or in other words, the individual is his/her life-history, and as far as this can be remembered, it is the individual concept the individual has of him- or herself. The order of time can be overcome in those special moments of remembrance in which the Past seems existent once more by being rooted in a present sensation. In these moments the individual experiences a timeless self. He continues (Vol. 3: 904–905):

> A moment of the past, did I say? Was it not perhaps very much more: something that, common both to the past and to the present, is much more essential than either of them? So often, in the course of life, reality had disappointed me because at the instant when my senses perceived it my imagination, which was the only organ that I possessed for enjoyment and beauty, could not apply itself to it, in virtue of that ineluctable law which ordains that we can only imagine what is absent. And now, suddenly, the effect of this harsh law had been neutralized, temporarily annulled, by a marvelous expedient of nature which had caused a sensation – the noise made both by the spoon and by the hammer, for instance – to be mirrored at one and the same time in the past, so that my imagination was permitted to savor it, and in the present, where the actual shock to my senses of the noise, the touch of the linen napkin, or whatever it might be, had added to the dreams of the imagination the concept of "existence" which they usually lack, and through this subterfuge had made it possible for my being to secure, to isolate, to immobilize – for a moment brief as a flash of lightening – what normally it never apprehends: a fragment of time in the pure state. The being which had been reborn in me when with a sudden shudder of happiness I had heard the noise that was common to the spoon touching the plate and the hammer striking the wheel, or had felt, beneath my feet, the unevenness that was common to the paving-stones of the Guermantes courtyard and to those of the baptistery of St. Mark's, this being is nourished only by the essences of things, in these alone does it find its sustenance and delight. In the observation of the present, where the senses cannot feed it with this food, it languishes, as it does in the consideration of the past made arid by the intellect or in the anticipation of a future which the will constructs with fragments of the present and the past, fragments whose reality it still further reduces by preserving of them only what is suitable for the utilitarian, narrowly human purpose for which it intends them. But let a noise or a scent, once heard or once smelt, be heard or smelt again in the present and at the same time in the past, real without being actual, ideal without being abstract, and immediately the permanent and habitually concealed essence of things is liberated and our true self, which seemed – to be dead but was not altogether dead, is awakened and reanimated as it receives the celestial nourishment that is brought to it. A minute freed from the order of time has

> re-created in us, to feel it, the man freed from the order of time. And one can understand that this man should have confidence in his joy, even if the simple taste of a madeleine does not seem logically to contain within it the reasons for his joy, one can understand that the word "death" should have no meaning for him; situated outside time, why should he fear the future?
> But this optical illusion which placed beside me a moment of the past that was incompatible with the present, could not last for long.

What is meant by the phrase "the essences of things"? It is that what is common to several experiences and what, to the Narrator, suddenly seems to be experienced in an enhanced state of consciousness. The generalizations, or essences, meant here, are not the ones that come about by generalizing over the perceptions of situations that are restricted by the perspectives of the everyday actions in which they are embedded ("preserving of them only what is suitable for the utilitarian, narrowly human purpose"), like the normal types or concepts, which Bergson has made the center of his theory of perception and concept formation. The generalizations over sensations and impressions Proust is after are mostly not expressed by the linguistic expressions coined in their standard use within action-guided concept formation. We have no words for the generalizations Proust is after, because they are not in the focus of inter-subjective attention in normal linguistic exchange, dominated by everyday actions and goals. We have no ready-coined words for representing these generalizations or concepts. We only can have these "essences" in re-living them in (series of) episodes that represent them. Since they are not those general concepts that are linguistically encoded and are normally represented by the respective words, the author has to make special efforts to tune us up towards employing them. This happens by very elaborate descriptions of scenes and episodes seen from out the Narrators special perspectives. These concepts or essences are for us only represented by the concrete real instances or examples. To the Narrator the instance, the sensation or impression in its similarity relationship to other instances, seems to be the idea or concept of the kind of sensation itself, formed by himself and now reproduced by himself, not just as an isolated example but as an example in a series of examples, in which Time is regained in the timelessness of the general concept or kind (type) of impression.

In the theory of Dynamic Conceptual Semantics, such series of situations or episodes are representations of a general concept or type, which by itself is not more than an equivalence class of such series of examples, namely of similarity sets, which are equivalent in the sense that when uniting them together into larger sets the similarity measure remains stable. However, a concept, idea, or type is not part of our consciousness. We rather experience the series of examples, which are concept representations, of which we can be, and are made conscious of in the course of the novel. Only in the episodes of the novel we become conscious of these series as concept representations, which form the course of the Narrator's life-history, as he tells it and puts it into perspectives.

In the mentalist tradition of Philosophy, concepts were assumed to exist as a special kind of mental entities, since understanding a situation does not seem to be possible without the essences (concepts, ideas), which capture what is common to the instances of the concepts. Also Proust's terminology about "essences" and "ideas" still is part of this tradition, although his method of recovering essences, ideas, and laws in the episodic composition of his novel gives no independent status to these. They only can appear in their concrete examples. The concept or idea is bound as a discriminating aspect within each example of it, namely within the episodes of the similarity set or series that form a representation of the concept. The idea can only show itself in its instances. It is not identical with its instance, though it can only be experienced in the instance. By experiencing two episodes, the present one and the past one, in close experiential connectedness by similarity, and in being aware also of their contrast, the common aspect, their identity, can be isolated by abstracting, for a moment, from the otherwise contrasting scenes. This identical aspect, here a concrete sensation experienced by itself in momentary isolation, is not a theoretical abstraction from the two scenes, though it is ideal because it is understood as common to both episodes. As a concrete sensation it is experienced as real, and hereby the past episode has a root in the present situation and is, as a whole, felt to be real for a moment. It is the phenomenal qualities or sensory-motor activity that makes from an idea or concept a concrete sensation.

When we say that an essence or idea or concept shows itself in its instances, we speak as if we accept an independent existence of these abstract entities. We rather should say that an idea or concept only exists in its instances, not simply in a realistic sense, but as a result of an interaction between objects, events, and our capacities to experience and understand them. This is a capacity of our brain and our body as a whole. There is no hidden mind in us in which concepts, without being conscious, exist. Rather there are in the brain groups of neurons which function, when activated, as conceptual indicators by virtue of their connections to other such indicators and their connections with sensorial, motor, emotional, and proprioceptual fields, and the causal bounds of these via our bodily organs to objects and events in our surroundings. When conceptual indicators are involved in circuit activation with the sensory-motor and emotional fields, we experience an episode as it is conceptualized, or aspectualized, by the conceptual indicators involved. By comparing several episodes that are partially conceptualized in the same way, we recognize the aspects that are common to them. We experience in this way the results of our capacity to conceptualize and understand our world, and the structure of the whole novel exteriorizes our own essence, namely our capability to perceive, imagine and understand a world according to how our brain is grown in biological development and in previous experiencing, which has caused learning processes and their results in terms of forming the whole connectivity of the brain. The life-history of the Narrator presented in the novel, as it is structured by the Narrator himself, is at the same time an expression of his capacity, as a special human being, of his ways of experiencing and conceptualizing the world, whereby it becomes his world, a possible world created in the novel.

The circuit activation between conceptual indicators and the sensory and motor and proprioception fields creates the experience, namely a conscious result, an impression or an episode. Furthermore, the past episode is not bound within the current purposes, and thus is free to be enjoyed as just what it is, which also causes aesthetic enjoyment, because of its freedom from the selectivity caused by the perspectives given in the current practical purposes. This makes it possible to experience a situation or object for its own sake and to experience the freedom of one's own cognitive activity in this act of experiencing, as Kant has pointed out. Brouwer (2003) has worked out how Kant's theory of imagination can show us how the formation of subjective, often metaphorically created concepts can lead to aesthetic enjoyment and can be intersubjective, and even universal, as far as imagination has a common ground in our cognitive abilities and in common ways of life.

The sensation by itself is not what is so essential for us. Rather that the sensation is related in contiguity to other parts of the respective situations in which it occurs makes it an essential link which establishes these situations as episodes that are part of our life, part of the timeless order of the reality that makes up our existence. Hereby we find ourselves in our self-consciousness as what we are, namely as our conceptually ordered life-history. The past, our unconscious self, is revealed to us in the remembered episodes presented within the orders established on them in concept formation, which makes up our understanding of ourselves as a being that has lived and that is living in the world in certain ways, in "ways of life", to speak with Wittgenstein.

Like the Narrator in these situations of remembrance, also the especially sensible child he had been had the ability to withdraw from being involved in the purposes of daily life and was able to concentrate on the aesthetic qualities and forms found in his surroundings, without always experiencing them merely as strictly bound into the normal ontological categorization of things and actions. Being attentive to the sensory and motor aspects of situations, without having them attentively embedded into ontological conceptualization, is only possible if the ontologically categorizing maps in our brain get not fully activated in perception. This can happen when much brain-energy is used up for activations within and between the emotional, sensorial, and proprioceptual systems. The activation circuits in the sensorial systems, in this case not being incorporated into the larger activation circuits including ontological conceptual indicators, produce conscious experiences that are enjoyed for themselves, without being totally merged into the perception of situations and things, characterized as such and such, and identified as particular situations and objects within their surroundings. In the aesthetically sensible child – re-constructed from memory by the Narrator when writing down his life-history – a lot of his energy is dedicated to the sensorial, proprioception, motor and emotion systems, and less energy to the areas of ontological conceptual indicators, which bind the impressions together into things, action and situations. The sensorial systems are not changed much through life, though finer differentiations between sensorial concepts can be learned or divided out in time, as well as contiguity patterns between them. They can get stabilized early on and are not much influenced by knowledge and everyday practices acquired later in life. But knowledge and routines become so dominant in the course of adapting to normal life that the sensorial systems just never do get activated without at the same time being part of the extended activation circuits involved in the higher cognitive faculties of general concepts and normal action routines. Thus, aesthetic enjoyment of sensations and their similarity and contiguity orderings, does not come about in normal daily life. It is left to artists to create it, like it has happened in impressionistic art, discussed in Proust's novel, and then further in expressionistic art (cf. Zeki 1999), where the systems of ontological categories where repressed in favor of the categories of the visual, emotional, and later also other sensorial and motor systems, as we find it in forms of motor art and installation art, which combines these systems and also re-introduces ontological concepts, exemplified in objects, in a metaphorical use or as ways to initiate certain imagined and partly performed unusual activities.

Proust points out that, in contrast to spontaneous remembering, recollecting scenes from the memory at will is something quite different from what he has experienced in these kinds of involuntary remembrances, which are especially rich in aesthetic quality. Also in this kind of involuntary remembering the memory conceptualizes the situation, which means that the situation is understood as a special episode. But hereby also something else is going on. The self with all its current interests is not involved within the context steering the conceptualization, or aspectualization, of the previous, recollected situation. Rather this past situation is re-lived with emphasis on its sensorial qualities. This means that in the aspectualization the aesthetic qualities are selected. There is no judgement or evaluation under present purposes intended, which would require the goal-directedness and controlling activity of the reflective self, which is conscious of itself, its position and its interests in the world. All this, on the other hand is involved in conceptualizing the actual, the present, scene. The Narrator writes (Vol. 3:906):

> And of course my memory had affirmed that each one of these sensations was quite unlike the others, though in fact all it was doing was to make various patterns out of elements that were homogeneous. But my recent experience of the three memories was something utterly different. These, on the contrary, instead of giving me a more flattering idea of myself, had almost caused me to doubt the reality, the existence of that self. And just as on the day when I had dipped the madeleine in the hot tea, in the setting of the place where I happened at the time to be – on that first day in my room in Paris, today at this moment the library of the Prince de Guermantes, a few minutes earlier the courtyard of this house – there had been inside me, a sensation (the taste of the madeleine dipped in the tea, a metal sound, a step of a certain kind) which was common both to my actual surroundings and also to another place (my aunt Leonie's bedroom, the railway carriage, the baptistery of St. Mark's), and now again, at the very moment when I was making these reflections, the shrill noise of water running through a pipe, a noise exactly like those long-drawn-out whistles which sometimes on summer evenings one heard the pleasure-steamers emit as they approached Balbec from the sea, made me feel – what I had once before made to feel in Paris, in a big restaurant, by the sight of a luxurious dining-room, half-empty, summery and hot – something that was not merely a sensation analogous to the one I used to have at the end of the afternoon in Balbec when ... It was no mere analogous sensation nor even a mere echo or replica of a past sensation that I was made to feel by the noise of the water in the pipe, it was that past sensation itself.

Note that here we have not two scenes or sensations that are consciously compared and judged as similar or identical. Rather the special past sensation and the special present sensation are experienced as one and the same. The past sensation is again part of the experiencing subject, and the present sensation is again part of the subject's now suddenly experiencing the past episode. There is no comparison of the Present with the Past and no judgment concerning the

Past, rather part of the Past is here again, re-lived in the Present. The Narrator continues:

> And in this case as in all the others, the sensation common to past and present had sought to re-create the former scene around itself, while the actual scene which had taken the former one's place opposed with all the resistance of material inertia this incursion into a house in Paris of a Normandy beach or a railway embankment. The marine dining-room of Balbec, with its damask linen prepared like so many altar cloths to receive the setting sun, had sought to shatter the solidity of the Guermantes mansion, to force open its doors, and for an instant had made the sofas around me sway and tremble as on another occasion it done to the tables of the restaurant in Paris. Always, when these resurrections took place, the distant scene engendered around the common sensation had for a moment grappled, like a wrestler, with the present scene. Always the present scene had come off victorious, and always the vanquished one had appeared to me the more beautiful one of the two, so beautiful that I had remained in a state of ecstasy on the uneven paving-stones or before the cup of tea, endeavoring to prolong or to reproduce the momentary appearances of the Combray or the Balbec or the Venice which invaded only to be driven back, which rose up only to at once to abandon me in the midst of the new scene which somehow, nevertheless, the past had been able to permeate. ... for so complete are these resurrections of the past during the seconds that they last, that they do not only oblige our eyes to cease to see the room which is near them in order to look instead at the railway bordered with trees or the rising tide, they even force our nostrils to breathe the air of places which are in fact a great distance away, and our will to choose between the various projects which those distant places suggest to us, they force our whole self to believe that it is surrounded by these places or at lest to waver doubtfully between them and the places where we now are, in a dazed uncertainty such as we feel sometimes when an indescribable beautiful vision presents itself to us at the moment of our falling asleep.   (Vol. 3:908)

The past scene in this kind of involuntary remembering does not function in the context of interests and goals of the Present. The aesthetic experience is the pleasure of re-living the Past, "the only genuine and fruitful pleasure I had known" (p. 908). From out this root in the Present the past episode grows and is re-lived and its contiguity relationships with its old surroundings and situations experienced there let these be re-lived too. The aesthetic pleasure grows with re-living a richer part of the Past:

> My exaltation and my joy grew steadily greater as probed more and more deeply into the noise of the spoon on the plate or the taste of the tea which

had been brought into my bedroom in Paris the bedroom of my aunt Léonie
and in its train all Combray and the two ways of our walks.   (p. 909)

This phenomenological description has a correspondence in the model of cognitively relevant circuit activity in the brain, which we employ here, following
the explorations on consciousness in Bartsch (2002), which were based on the
requirements of a dynamic conceptual semantics and the formal properties of
connectionist models, on the one hand side, and on neurological models of the
visual system, the blindsight phenomena, and dynamic models of brain activity on the other side. This model of consciousness, which claims that circuit
activation with involvement of sensorial and motor areas is the basis of consciousness, is supported, among others, also by empirical studies by Lamme
(from 1995 to 2003), who claims that a one-directional activation from out a
sensory stimulus to the conceptual areas does not result in consciousness, as
long as there is no recurrent activation from out the conceptualizing fields,
though such a sensory input can also cause further reactions in the motor
system, or reactions as known from the blindsight cases. Thus one can, for
example react adequately while driving a car on the motorway, although one
is not always conscious of the situation on the road, to which one nevertheless is informationally sensitive. In our model of consciousness, the following
brain processes would be a parallel to, and a causal background for, involuntary
remembrance.

The Narrator's observations concerning the relationship between the
present situation and the remembered one can be explained in terms of competing, but partly overlapping circuit activations. The activation of circuits
within and between the concept indicators on the conceptual and routine
fields, the sensorial and motor systems, in which sensorial concept indicators
interact in activation circuits with the primary sensorial, motor, emotional,
and proprioceptual fields, lets emerge the experiences in consciousness as being of a certain type and feeling. The present episodic experience fits into the
series of previous experiences in which this type of sensation was instantiated,
and in this way the old sensation is now felt again. But the activation circuits
due to the present context are merely connectively associated with those of the
present situation and enhance this one, selecting or emphasizing there what
is relevant in this context. The circuits of the present episode, aspectualized in
this manner, compete with the activity circuits of the remembered scene, which
are induced and enforced by the memory indices. This gives rise to the competition and alternation of the present episode with the remembered one, as
Proust describes it.

The "essence of things", as it comes about in the interaction between our subjective capacity of concept formation and the world, does not merely lie in the identity of past and present sensations, but also in the contiguity of these sensations with the surrounding experiences, which can be re-lived in this connectedness. In this connectedness the "essences" lie within our selves, our conceptual, emotional and habitual make-up, which we have built up from childhood onwards by interacting with our natural and social surroundings. In this way they are personal, though publicly guided in many ways, but the author lets us take part in his subjectivity by letting the Narrator unravel and demonstrate them in the connectedness of the episodes in the novel.

The aesthetic pleasure had not been felt in the original experience of the remembered episode. Then it was bound within the context in attention to all the practical purposes and also those aspects of the episode or situations that were functional at that moment. But now in remembrance, due to a new contrasting practical context, the episode is divided out and is thus free from that previous selective practical context. The episode is now experienced without the purposes that were dominant then. This frees the sensory impressions from their ontological bond within objects and actions such that they can be enjoyed freely for what they are by themselves, or rather for what they are according to our free-wheeling cognitive capacities, when these are not restricted by the normal perspectives of daily life. Here Proust makes use of an insight of classical Kantian aesthetics. This is also the reason why willful remembrance of the old episodes, or remembrance initiated by a similarity in the ontological aspects, namely the kinds of things and actions involved, does not result in aesthetic enjoyment. In such a voluntary remembrance the episode more likely comes back in its old form, selected for ontological conceptualization in its normal everyday guise.

The Narrator asks himself how he could use these experiences for his writing:

> To this contemplation of the essence of things I had decided therefore that in future I must attach myself, so as somehow to immobilize it. But how, by what means, was I to do it?   (p. 909)

He points out that going back to the old places does not bring back Time Lost. Just composing willfully the memories does not do it:

> Experience had taught me only too well the impossibility of attaining in the real world to what lay deep within myself; I knew that Lost Time was not to be found again on the piazza of St. Mark's anymore than I had found it again on my second visit to Balbec or on my return to Tansonville....   (p. 911)

This aesthetic pleasure could not come from the impressions from the outside. It is also not found in the original experiences in Combray, or in Balbec. The Narrator goes on

> I had not known pleasure in Balbec any more than I had known pleasure when I lived with Albertine, for the pleasure of living with her had been perceptible to me only in retrospect. When I recapitulated the disappointments of my life as a lived life … I saw clearly that the disappointments of travel and the disappointments of love were not different disappointments at all but the varied aspects which are assumed, according to the particular circumstances which bring it into play, by our inherent powerlessness to realize ourselves in material enjoyment or in effective action. And thinking again of the extra-temporal joy which I had been made to feel by the sound of the spoon or the taste of the madeleine, I said to myself: "Was this perhaps that happiness which the little phrase of the sonata promised to Swann and which he, because he was unable to find it in artistic creation, mistakenly assimilated to the pleasures of love, was this the happiness of which long ago I was given a presentiment – as something more supra-terrestrial even than the mood evoked by the little phrase of the sonata – by the call, the mysterious, rubescent call of that septet which Swann was never privileged to hear, having died like so many others before the truth that was made for him had been revealed?   (p. 911)

Swann had not the experiences necessary for making him a writer or an artist. He was an able critic, but lacked the power of creation. The critic, when informing about and when evaluating a work of art, is for a large part also involved with himself, with presenting himself to the readers in favorable terms. This is a context of interests and practical purposes, which selects everything from the work of art that is adequate within this context. But it does not provide the free space in which the work of art can be experienced in its essential aesthetic quality. – This, of course, also holds for writing a study like the present one.

Already the young child enjoyed aesthetic experiences on walks around Combray, when his sensitivity was not fully embedded within the practical purposes of daily life and within the need to present himself to his social surroundings. When he was freely striving around, he felt aesthetic joy, without yet having all these remembrances of past scenes. It seems that here he enjoys the working of basic ordering principles of concept formation, similarity and association in contiguity, activated when experiencing the world around him. In neurological terms, the creation of activation circuits, in ordering the sensations according to similarity (generalization) and contiguity (association), the competition of circuits in the process of aspectualizing the experiences, and the short term stabilization of some of them working together in certain rhythms due to frequencies of neuronal firing, result in a short time equilibrium of the cognitive processes, which might cause the aesthetic joy alongside with the resulting experience of a scene or episode in early years. The Narrator informs us about this in the following way (Vol. 3:912):

> And then, after I had dwelt for some time upon these resurrections of memory, the thought came to me that in another fashion certain obscure impressions, already even at Combray on the Guermantes way, had solicited my attention in a fashion somewhat similar to these reminiscences, except that they concealed within them not a sensation dating from an earlier time, but a new truth, a precious image which I had sought to uncover by efforts of the same kind as those that we make to recall something that we have forgotten, as if our finest ideas were like tunes, which as it were, come back to us although we have never heard them before and which we have to make an effort to hear and to transcribe.

He had made effort to encipher some hidden truth in impressions and images, but this is not an effort of the intellect:

> For the truths which the intellect apprehends directly in the world of full and unimpeded light have something less profound, less necessary than those which life communicates to us against our will in an impression which is material because it enters us through the senses but yet has a spiritual meaning which it is possible for us to extract. In fact, both in the one case and in the other, whether I was concerned with impressions like the one which I had received from the sight of the steeples of Martinville or with reminiscenses like that of the unevenness of the two steps or the taste of the madeleine, the task was to interpret the given sensations as signs of so many laws and ideas, by trying to think – that is to say, to draw forth from the shadow – what I had merely felt, by trying to convert it into its spiritual equivalent. And this method, which seemed to me the sole method, what was it but the creation of a work of art?
>
> (p. 912)

Such a root-sensation apparently functions as a pointer to the situations of which it is part, and hereby to the suitable situational concepts, the type of the situation (the law or idea), which is exemplified in different ways throughout the novel, or throughout the life of the Narrator. The "laws" or "essences", being the situational types or concepts, become conscious to us only via their examples, the episodes or situations pointed at by the sensation initiating their remembrance. The sensations and connected episodes are the material for the writer to exemplify and illustrate in modified details the types of life-situations. In the novel, the situational concepts, or types, get represented by describing their examples, the instances of a type. These are the concrete episodes and situations. But it is not only the situational and sensorial concepts or types, represented through their examples. Rather the whole cognitive activity itself is enjoyed in its results, in the order found and created. The method, also the method of creation of a work of art, is here the ordering of impressions according to similarity and (different kinds of) contiguity, in its dependence on motor activity and the whole emotional and bodily context, and generally in its dependence on different perspectives. This method, employed unconsciously by the subject, organizes our world as we experience it and shows itself in the order existing between its results. The author makes use of this method, partly unconscious, and exhibits it in a conscious and controlled way in the structure of the whole novel. In fact, this method is the method of concept formation generally taking place unconsciously, but here drawn into consciousness in the structure of the novel.

The method of the writer, at least the one of the genius, is not to start from hypotheses and design experiments to prove or disprove them, but he starts with impressions, images which are given and in which he reveals laws and ideas, order, by just letting the powers of the mind work on them to create concept formation and understanding by weaving through his descriptions of episodes a network of similarities, contrasts, and contiguity in relationships that come up in association. This is not working in intended directions, as it would be in perception that is guided by actions of everyday ways of life. Rather it is freely following patterns, musical phrases, themes composed of impressions and sensations, which are found in experienced situations. These have not been abstracted from situations by the normal process of concept formation guided by linguistic order like relationships in structural semantics or by goal-directed actions, whereby the context of everyday necessities creates the inter-subjectively current perspectives, or attention-spaces, under which the normal, inter-subjectively guided concept formation and understanding takes place. It rather is exploring the unconscious, the potentiality of our mind for forming generalizations (concepts, ideas, laws) on all kinds of situational experiences, also under unusual perspectives, and hereby understanding the situations by being able to distinguish aspects in them and see their relationships to other situations, which are not the common, normalized, ones. At the same time this process is the creation of a new, somewhat other world for us, which is built from the same material and by the same cognitive processes in concept formation as is our normal world, but the cognitive operations are applied under other and unusual perspectives. This potentiality of our mind is set out by the categorizing and associating connective powers of our brain, the cognitive capacity of concept formation and understanding in its broadest sense, encompassing emotional, sensorial, proprioception and motor activity in interaction with the general and especially the specific memory about individuals and episodes. Hereby also the conceptual indicators of aesthetic types or concepts, like the musical, choreographic, and literary phrases found in cultural products but also in movements and compositions in natural surroundings, are employed or built up in the unconscious process of repeated and new experiencing, in interaction with the indices of the specific memory, namely the indices of individual concepts and the episodes.

We can interpret Proust's reflections on the method of the writer in the following way. To make the method of the unconscious itself present in consciousness in presenting a work of art by showing the creation of the work of art, this is what Proust does in his novel. In this novel, the Narrator shows us, and reflects on, the process of writing the very novel. The process of creation by the artist is the topic of the creation itself. What is called "essences", "laws", "truths" are the generalizations, the concepts and habits or routines and the dispositions of emotional reactions, and the inter-relationships and interactions between these laws or concepts and the specific memories and the sensory impressions and motor activities. In fact, the whole novel is the phenomenological emergence of a mind-full reality from the brain that is formed in its full capacity by the history of body and brain in their surroundings. Here not just facts and episodes are (re-)produced, rather the ways, and especially the growth of concept formation and understanding, as it is grounded in the unconscious brain activity, is shown in the only matter in which something can be shown, namely in the episodic ways of consciousness. Concept formation, which at the same time is growing understanding, is shown in the way in which the episodes, images, impressions are presented, newly created, or based on past experiences. Besides this general growth of our understanding of the world in its repetitions and modifications, special, unusual perspectives are opened up as the attention spaces that are not induced by our normal, willful manner of action. These perspectives are not called up in willful actions or are intentionally called up directly, rather they are introduced by a sensory-motor experience, which like a spark gives light to a whole new extra perspective, under which aspects of situations appear that become salient details for the subject and are seen as pointing to other similar episodes. These episodes or situations are similar in that they contain the same aspects, and by collecting these similar situations together, a new concept is formed, or an old concept is represented.

In the formation of a new concept these aspects now get indicated by an indicator, which is established in the subject's brain in experiencing these situations. We thus have a series of situations that represents the newly established concept or type, which is, for the subject, the 'essence' of these situations. But in the unconscious brain of the subject, with such an essence there corresponds not more than just a conceptual indicator, a group of neurons with its connections to other such indicators and to the sensory-motor fields, the emotion fields and the proprioception fields. The 'essence', or the concept, shows itself in consciousness only within the instances, when they are seen under the new perspective, which provides the conceptual space in which they can be seen. The concept or 'essence' formed in this way is subjective in as far as it is not yet inter-subjectively shared. It is the task of the writer to present the situations and episodes such that within the reader a sensibility is created and perspectives are taken that can make him share the experiences and make also him form these concepts, and hereby make him share the world of the Narrator in *A la recherche du temps perdu*.

The Narrator is not free in what he experiences. The unconscious cognitive processes of concept formation and understanding, and what they have built up as orderings in his brain, hold him in their grip when he experiences situations. At the same time they are what makes his very special self, his cognitive capacity. They are part of what he is, and of that we are not conscious.

> Already the consequences came flooding into my mind: whether I considered reminiscences of the kind evoked by the noise of the spoon or the taste of the madeleine, or those truths written with the aid of shapes for whose meaning I searched in my brain, where – church steeples or wild grass growing in a wall – they composed a magical scrawl, complex and elaborate, their essential character was that I was not free to choose them, that such as they were they were given to me. And I realized that this must be the mark of their authenticity.
>
> (p. 913)

This realization is typical for an experience of emergence of some episode triggered by a part of it that has been sensed. Connective activity between conceptual indicators and memory indices and the process leading to the emergence of an episode is something of which we are not conscious; it merely can be shown and thus indirectly become conscious in its results, in series of episodes and in acts of contemplation about episodes, impressions, activities, images. It requires an attitude of self-consciousness directed at oneself as a perceiver, and not merely directed at the perceived. The Narrator tries to direct his own and our attention towards that what has been attributed to the impressions by his own mind, or rather by the connective activity between conceptual indicators and the sensorial, motor, emotional and proprioception fields in the brain, and thus creates the awareness of the special character but also of the generality of what he perceives, and/or imagines.

> I had not gone in search of the two uneven paving-stones of the courtyard on which I had stumbled. But it was precisely the fortuitous and inevitable fashion in which this and the other sensations had been encountered that proved the trueness of the past which they brought back to life, of the images which they released, since we feel, with these sensations, the effort that they make to climb back towards the light, feel in ourselves the joy of rediscovering what is real. And here too was the proof of the trueness of the whole picture formed out of those contemporaneous impressions which the first sensation brings back in its train, with those unerring proportions of light and shade, emphasis and omission, memory and forgetfulness to which conscious recollection and conscious observation will never know how to attain.   (p. 913)

"Conscious recollection and observation" here means willful, voluntarily intended recollection and observation, which always is formed by selecting those aspects that are relevant for the present context and purpose of the act of remembrance and observation. Also the truth, or the essence, at issue here in involuntary remembrance is what has been achieved by the general conceptual, habitual, emotional capacities that are involved in re-creating the episode by interacting with the sensorial, emotional, proprioception and motor fields. But these capacities here, in this moment of stumbling over the uneven paving stones, are not restricted by the present practical context which triggers certain intentions and hereby causes restricting selections on the fields of cognitive activity; and these capacities are also not hampered by an overflow of distracting impressions of all kind from the outside, which would hinder the sensory-motor activation triggered from out the conceptual indicators, whereby the episode can arise in its phenomenal qualities in remembrance. Furthermore the practical present context for the moment does not hinder the free contemplation on a certain episode or scene. The workings of the conceptual indicators in their relationships to each other, induced by previous episodes and their recurring parts and relations, are what the writer is going to explore. Since we are not conscious about them, we only can find concepts, or essences, instantiated in the episodes in which they are manifested. The Narrator expresses it like this:

> As for the inner book of unknown symbols (symbols carved in relief they might have been, which my attention, as it explored my unconscious, groped for and stumbled against and followed the contours of, like a diver exploring the ocean-bed), if I tried to read them no one could help me with any rules, for to read them was an act of creation in which no one can do our work for us or even collaborate with us. How many for this reason turn aside from writing!

What tasks do men not take upon themselves in order to evade this task! Every
public event, be it the Dreyfus case, be it the war, furnishes the writer with a
fresh excuse for not attempting to decipher this book: he wants to assure the
triumph of justice, he wants to restore the moral unity of the nation, he has no
time to think of literature. But these are mere excuses, the truth being that he
has not or no longer has genius, that is to say instinct. For instinct dictates our
duty and the intellect supplies us with pretexts for evading it. But excuses have
no place in art and intentions count for nothing: at every moment the artist
has to listen to his instinct, and it is this that makes art the most real of all
things, the most austere school of life, the true last judgment. This book, more
laborious to decipher than any other, is also the only one which has been dic-
tated to us by reality, the only one of which the "impression" has been printed
in us by reality itself. (p. 914)

Concept formation in us is guided by truth and norm from outside us, namely
by reality and by inter-subjective goals and expectations. If the latter is excluded or left behind, then reality in its general features and relationships could
guide concept formation as the sole external factor, besides our cognitive, emotional, and sensory-motor capacities. Reality provides us with impressions that
contain the general features we are able to grasp by an interaction of our capacities, including the conceptual ordering already established on the series of
previous impressions. The understanding of each new impression depends on
the ordering established on previous data. Proust continues lining out concept
formation:

When an idea – an idea of any kind – is left in us by life, its material pattern,
the outline of the impression that it made upon us, remains behind as a to-
ken of its necessary truth. The ideas formed by pure intelligence have no more
than a logical, a possible truth, they are arbitrarily chosen. The book whose
hieroglyphs are patterns not traced, is the only book that belongs to us. Not
that the ideas that we form by ourselves cannot be correct in logic; that they
may well be, but we cannot know whether they are true. Only the impression,
however trivial its material may seem to be, however faint its traces, is a criterion of truth and deserves for that reason to be apprehended by the mind, for
the mind, if it succeeds in extracting this truth, can by the impression and by
nothing else be brought to a state of greater perfection and given a pure joy.
The impression is for the writer what experiment is for the scientist, with the
difference that in the scientist the work of the intelligence precedes the experiment and in the writer it comes after the impression. What we have not had to
decipher, to elucidate by our own efforts, what was clear before we looked at
it, is not ours. From ourselves comes only that which we drag forth from the
obscurity which lies within us, that which to others is unknown. (p. 914)

This "book of hieroglyphs" is the map of our potential mind, is the whole of our dispositions to act, to feel, and to understand; it is the set of the conceptual conditions of all our possible experience, of episodes and situations we can encounter due to the order of similarity and contiguity established in our brain on the set of all our past experiences. This order in us, the unconscious, our own identity, is experienced and shown in what we are conscious of, namely in the episodes that form our life-history. It "has been printed in us by reality itself."

> I had arrived then at the conclusion that in fashioning a work of art we are by no means free, that we do not choose how we shall make it but that it pre-exists us and therefore we are obliged, since it is both necessary and hidden, to do what we should have to do if it were a law of nature, that is to say to discover it. But this discovery which art obliges us to make, is it not, I thought, really the discovery of what, though it ought to be more precious to us than anything else in the world, yet remains ordinarily for ever unknown to us, the discovery of our true life, of reality as we have felt it to be, which differs so greatly from what we think it is that when a chance happening brings us an authentic memory of it we are filled with an immense happiness? In this conclusion I was confirmed by the thought of the falseness of so-called realistic art, which would not be so untruthful if we had not in life acquired the habit of giving to what we feel a form of expression which differs so much from, and which we nevertheless after a little time take to be, reality itself.   (p. 915)

The laws, essences, general truths are in us, hidden in our (unconscious) memory; it is the conceptual system that we have established in the course of our life-history. Every situation, thing, book or work of art can only be understood within the context then around us, and on the background of the conceptual system (including habits, routines, emotional and evaluative capacities) developed so far in our life-history. Proust puts it like this:

> A thing which we saw, a book which we read at a certain period does not merely remain for ever conjoined to what existed then around us; it remains also faithfully united to what we ourselves then were and thereafter it can be handled only by the sensibility, the personality that were then ours.   (p. 921)

This side of reality that is in us, and that is what the author is after, is not so much expressed by the concepts expressed in normal linguistically guided forms of life, by the common coins of daily exchange, rather this side of our reality more concerns the subjective personality as it is formed by its personal history, which does not find expression in normal everyday conversation, but nevertheless exhibits general types and laws. And these laws are the ones that make up the structure of our sensibility, our personal ways of experiencing, feeling, and enacting our roles within our surroundings. They thus are those general concepts or types that are part of the sensory-motor, emotional and emphatic, and proprioceptual systems. The neural indicators of these concepts order and structure the perceptive, imaginative, motor and emotional activities on the respective primary sensorial and motor fields within these systems, and thus give rise to episodes emerging in our consciousness. Proust thinks that there are general concepts or patterns that, formed early in life, stay identical throughout our whole life, though they are re-modeled and modified in specific details through our history. Deep traces formed in childhood mold the experiences later in life such that they fall into the same pattern. But there is also change of concepts, and new concepts and understanding due to modifications caused by later experiences. Conceptual indicators established in our life-history, a history of learning, aspectualize or conceptualize a current episode such that it is experienced as identical in certain aspects or sensations with some previous episode, whereby the present episode then can be pushed aside in order for the previous one to be re-lived.

A flash into the Past by a momentary bodily sensation can bring back a previous episode only when much of the present ways of understanding, i.e. part of the conceptual system of present use is suppressed or de-activated. But it always remains doubtful whether what is remembered is really the old episode, or rather is a new version of the old episode, which is new, because the conceptual system is not the old one but has changed in the mean time. Thus, what the old Narrator writes about his childhood might be some other childhood than that what it had been. The greatest chance of coming close to the original is created when the developed ontological conceptual system of the adult, our kinds of objects and kinds of actions, activities and events, is somehow cut down in its role in understanding and when the old episodes are re-lived merely on the level of situational impressions which are categorized only on the basic categorizing systems of the modalities of perception, motor activity, and emotion.

Even then, as Proust's tells us, the old childhood episode was not the same as the remembered one, because it then had been selectively controlled by the leading purposes in those previous situations in which the child lived. But if the ontological categorizations of the old situation and of the current situation are cancelled against each other as the contrasting aspects, then what is common to them remains. Remaining are the aspects of sensory-motor, emotional and proprioceptual categorization. – This is the basic idea of impressionist art, and also later of expressionist art, where one tries to close off factual information and higher ontological categories (object, actions). The artist tries to push them into the background or makes them fuzzy and barely recognizable, such that impressions and emotions can be shown more purely with a minimum of conceptual categorization, namely with only the aspectualization (conceptualization, categorization) provided by the sensory-motor, emotional, and proprioceptual systems, leaving out the ontological categorizations of things, events, and actions. – This elimination of the standard ontological categorizations in perception is not possible in the normal courses of life, which are guided by interests and necessities of action to which the ontological characterizations are suitable. But an aesthetic orientation in creating and enjoying art, and experiencing the world under an aesthetic perspective will set free the aesthetic conceptualizations of situations and episodes. The emphasis Proust places on describing sensations, feelings, and situational impressions of early childhood is motivated by the same idea. Still, these episodes cannot be re-lived by intention; they have to be re-lived through the ignition by a real sensation, which is part of a present episode.

> And if I still possessed the *Francois le Champi* which Mamma unpacked one evening from the parcel of books which my grandmother was to have given me for my birthday, I should never look at it; I should be too afraid that I might gradually insinuate into it my impressions of today and smother my original impressions beneath them, that I might see it become so far a thing of the present that, when I ask it to evoke once more the child who spelt out its title in the little bedroom at Combray, the child, not recognizing its voice, would no longer reply to its summons and would remain for ever buried in oblivion.
>
> (p. 924)

Reality as it is for us, namely each situation we have understood, arises by a combination of memory and present sensation. This in fact is the principle of concept formation and understanding, which says that something is understood, or conceptualized, by being embedded into those similarity sets or series of previously experienced situations into which it fits best. These growing similarity sets, together with contiguity sets, form our conceptual system, the general memory. – In neurological terms, our general memory consists of conceptual indicators, namely groups of neurons, and their inter-connections and their connections to the sensory-motor and emotional fields. – The writer has, according to the Narrator, to reconstruct this joining together of sensations and memory. This means that he re-constructs the basic lines of the history of learning or concept formation of the subject, especially how new experiences fall into old series of similar and contiguous experiences, or how they begin to establish new orderings, new concepts, on the whole set of experiences of a life's history. Also aesthetic experiences are due to these embeddings and the experience of fitting of the new into the old. Also metaphoric ordering of data follows the method of embedding or linking an episode with one or more episodes on the basis of similarity and relational similarity (analogy). We have seen (cf. Bartsch 1998 and 2002b) that metaphorical concept formation and understanding is this linking or embedding operation taking place under a change to a new perspective, while normal concept formation and understanding keeps a previously and normally taken perspective constant along the series of examples seen as similar.

> An hour is not merely an hour, it is a vase full of scents and sounds and projects and climates, and what we call reality is a certain connection between these immediate sensations and the memories which envelop us simultaneously with them – a connection that is suppressed in a simple cinematographic vision, which just because it professes to confine itself to the truth in fact departs widely from it – a unique connection which the writer has to rediscover in order to link for ever in his phrase the two sets of phenomena which reality joins together. He can describe a scene by describing one after another the innumerable objects which at a given moment were present at a particular place, but truth will be attained by him only when he takes two different objects, states the connection between them – a connection analogous in the world of art to the unique connection which in the world of science is provided by the law of causality – and encloses them in the necessary links of a well-wrought style; truth – and life too – can be attained by us only, when, by comparing a quality common to two sensations, we succeed in extracting their common essence and in reuniting them to each other, liberated from the contingencies of time, within a metaphor. Had not nature herself – if one considered the matter from this point of view – placed me on the path of art, was she not herself a beginning of art, she who, often, had allowed me to become aware of the beauty of one thing only in another thing, of the beauty, for instance, of noon at Combray in the sounds of its bells, of that of the mornings at Doncieres in the hiccups of our central heating? The link may be uninteresting, the objects trivial, the style bad, but unless this process has taken place the description is worthless.
>
> (p. 924–925)

The immediate sensations are the roots in present reality by which the surrounding remembered episodes are felt to be part of reality again. The Narrator now reconstructs the experience of the identity of the present and the previous sensation as the result of an act of comparison: we compare two sensations and extract what is common to them. But that does not seem quite the way it works, he remarks. It cannot be just the normal descriptions we all would give of things and scenes, and the normal generalizations:

> But was it true that reality was not more than this? If one tries to understand
> what actually happens at the moment when a thing makes some particular
> impression upon one – on the day, for instance, when as I crossed the bridge
> over the Vivonne the shadow of a cloud upon the water had made me cry
> "Gosh!" and jump for joy.   (p. 925)

The rational reconstruction following the linguistically represented features
does not give the right picture of what happens when one experiences what
is common between two experienced episodes. What is common to several situational impressions can be unexpressed and even be inexpressible by standard
linguistic usage because this experience is not inter-subjectively shared and linguistically coded in language. What is common across several situations can be
rather personal, though it also can be experienced by others, if they are able to
share the personal history with the Narrator and thus share enough common
ground with the Narrator. And this is the point of presenting this history to the
public. The readers have to share the new, or at least not standard perspectives
of the Narrator, which he has developed during his life. These perspectives select other similarities than the usual ones. They are the similarities that create
the aesthetic experience. By following the experiences in the life-history of the
Narrator, the reader will hopefully be able to take part in his aesthetic experience. This cannot be reached by just focusing on what is inter-subjective and
objective ontological categorization in normal linguistic usage.

> Even where the joys of art are concerned, although we seek and value them for
> the sake of the impression that they give us, we contrive as quickly as possible
> to set aside, as being inexpressible, precisely that element in them which is
> the impression that we sought, and we concentrate instead upon that other
> ingredient in aesthetic emotion which allows us to savor its pleasure without
> penetrating its essence and lets us suppose we are sharing it with other art-
> lovers, with whom we find it possible to converse just because, the personal
> root of our own impression having been suppressed, we are discussing with
> them a thing which is the same for them and us.   (p. 927)

The subjective part of our experiences and knowledge, namely what the memory or the previously formed conceptual system of this special subject contributes to understanding of situations or objects, or books for that matter, is
partly inter-subjective, shared with others in its conceptual structures, as far as
it is based on common experiences in learning the common language in the
shared worldly surroundings. However for another part it also is purely subjective and can only be taken into account by others to the degree to which
they get to know the more peculiar episodes of the subject's life-history. The

Narrator's telling his story gives us the input necessary for understanding his world. He gives us part of his subjectivity, which is also contained (besides the normal inter-subjectively learned means of conceptualization) in the second part, which is conjoined with the sensation as the first part, in order to provide for an understanding of the situation presented.

> ...every impression is double and the one half which is sheathed in the object is prolonged in ourselves by another half which we alone can know, we speedily find means to neglect this second half, which is the one on which we ought to concentrate ...   (p. 927)

The specific personal structure of this second half, as Proust sees it, is negated in art criticism and description of the most knowledgeable and erudite writers on art. These personally specific conceptual structures of the second half can be revealed also to others by the ways in which episodes are composed in literary art, under the special perspectives that make us attentive to the sensory-motor and emotional qualities, by which aesthetic experience becomes possible. These non-normal perspectives provide for conceptualizing situations and episodes differently, and thus make up new experiences, which open up new worlds for us. Such specific personal conceptual structures, truly subjective ways of ordering and hereby forming experiences, are also found in the lives of other persons, though they have not been exhibited in concept formation guided by normal linguistic intercourse. By following the artistic expression of another person, in a poetic work, in painting or in music, we can take part in the special conceptual structures formed by the life of these other (artistic) persons and thus can follow new ways of structuring and understanding the data the world imposes on us. This means that we can take part in experiencing other worlds.

> But art, if it means awareness of our own life, meant also awareness of the lives of other people – for style for the writer, no less than color for the painter, is a question not of technique but of vision: it is the revelation, which by direct and conscious methods would be impossible, of the qualitative difference, the uniqueness of the fashion in which the world appears to each of us, a difference which, if there were no art, would remain for ever the secret of every individual. Through art alone we are able to emerge from ourselves, to know what another person sees of a universe which is not the same as our own and of which, without art, the landscapes would remain as unknown to us as those that may exist in the moon. Thanks to art, instead of seeing one world only, our own, we make that world multiply itself and we have at our disposal as many worlds as there are original artists, worlds more different one from the other then those which revolve in infinite space, worlds which, centuries after

> the extinction of the fire from which their light emanated, whether it is called
> Rembrandt or Vermeer, send us still each one its special radiance.   (p. 932)

The Narrator shows his way of understanding other persons, his ways of forming individual concepts of them. He further suggests that we all do it in that
manner. Hereby he lets us see how specific personal desires, expectations, prej-
udices and dispositions to act form the individual concept we have of another
person. In understanding other persons, we direct and project towards and
onto the other person our own cognitive, emotional, and emphatic abilities
and tendencies, and thus create these persons for us according to our own conditions. Albertine, by herself, seems to be a young woman without properties,
without a real character. The Narrator never really knew her well and also did
not take the effort to get to know her for her own sake. Rather he merely created
her as his companion and thus made her a prisoner not only by keeping her in
his house and guarding her ways by his jealous attention, but also by projecting
on her that she would behave in this or that manner, would want this or that,
and by getting her things of which he thought that she would like them, and by
trying to bind her by means of great presents, such that she would have to be
grateful to him. Albertine is the Narrator's creature, the object of his love and
obsessions, and she only becomes herself when she escapes, and hereby leaves
the Narrator's world for good.

Not only situations but also persons are the constructions out of two contributing factors, of sensations caused by reality in the Narrator, and of his typical expectations, wishes and pre-occupations, among these his general habits
and hopes of finding love and security.

> But I realized also that the suffering caused by the thought that our love does
> not belong to the person who inspires it, a suffering which I had first known
> in connection with Gilberte, is for two reasons salutary. ... But the principle
> reason is that, if our love is not only the love of a Gilberte (and this fact is what
> we find so painful), the reason is not that it is also the love of an Albertine, but
> that it is a portion of our mind more durable than the various selves which
> successively die within us and which would, in their egoism, like to keep it
> to themselves, a portion of our mind which must, however much it hurts us
> (and the pain may in fact be beneficial), detach itself from the individuals so
> that we can comprehend and restore to it its generality and give this love, the
> understanding of this love, to all, to the universal spirit, and not merely first
> to one woman and then to another with whom first one and then another of
> the selves that we have successively been has desired to be forever united.
> (Vol. 3: 933–934)

We see that a general concept in us, the idea or the law, is activated and expressed only in sequences of concrete examples in the course of one's life, here of the Narrator's love to his mother, to his grandmother, to Gilberte, to the Duchesse de Guermantes, and to Albertine. And such a general concept also determines how we build up an individual concept of a person. The series of the Narrator's loves is contrasted with a series of obsessions of other figures of the novel, such as Swann with Odette, Saint Loupe with Rachel, and Charlus with Morel. In exploring the identities and differences in series of examples, here situations characterized by the Narrator's or other figures' devotion, love, jealousy, obsession with respect to other women or men, the Narrator explores his, and generally the human possibilities, and hereby man's essential conditions of living in the natural and social world. These are the "laws" or dispositions, which make certain situations and episodes possible, and hereby also restrict the range of possibilities we have in life. They thus frame the set of possible worlds for us. This generality has to be shown in series of concrete episodes, which are, of course, part of a world that evolves according to normal laws of nature and society, and therefore can be described by our normal language and normal narrative devises, at least in so far that they are characterized and also identified as certain situations. By living or re-living these episodes in imagination we can also find common aspects that are not expressed in the descriptions. The linguistic descriptions of situations serve as skeletons on which imagination can provide the flesh, the general aesthetically relevant features that have no names, but that are experienced, remembered, or imagined and that are essential in the personal past life.

> I felt, however, that these truths which the intellect educes directly from reality were not altogether despised, for they might be able to enshrine within a matter less pure indeed but still embued with mind those impressions which are conveyed to us outside time by the essences that are common to the sensations of the past and of the present, but which, just because they are more precious, are also too rare for a work of art to be constructed exclusively from them, and – capable of being used for this purpose – I felt jostling each other within me a whole host of truths concerning human passions and character and conduct. The perception of these truths caused me joy; and yet I seemed to remember that more than one of them had been discovered by me in suffering, and others in very trivial pleasures (every individual who makes us suffer can be attached by us to a divinity of which he or she is a mere fragmentary reflection, the lowest step in the ascent that leads to it, a divinity or an Idea which, if we turn to contemplate it, immediately gives us joy instead of the pain which we were feeling before – indeed the whole art of living is to

make use of the individuals through whom we suffer as a step enabling us to draw nearer to the divine form which they reflect and thus joyously people our life with divinities). And then a new light, less dazzling, no doubt, than that other illumination which had made me perceive that the work of art was the sole means of discovering Lost Time, shone suddenly within me. And I understood that all these materials for a work of literature were simply my past life; I understood that they had come to me, in frivolous pleasures, in indolence, in tenderness, in unhappiness, and that I had stored them up without divining the purpose for which they were destined or even their continued existence any more than a seed does when it forms within itself a reserve of all the nutritious substances from which it will feed a plant.   (p. 935–936)

Time Lost, the whole of our previous experiences, has been solidified in our conceptual (including the perceptual, emotional and emphatic, the habitual, and the evaluation) systems of understanding, namely of conceptualizing our world, which is hereby formed in ordering our experiences according to the innate principles of concept formation. Hereby Time Lost seems to have become the timeless conceptual system of the subject. In concept formation and understanding we look for similarity and contiguity under various perspectives. Our innate and our acquired ways of conceptualizing under these perspectives are what is meant by the "essences", or "types", or "divinities" in us, which are our dispositions for acting and for ordering, that is conceptualizing, the impressions that persons, objects and situations make on us, such that we experience them in certain ways and such that we can act in certain ways. These ways can only be shown (in matter) by the Narrator's re-writing his life-history, and by especially attending to situations in which he suffers through others, whereby they reflect the conceptualizations he has projected on them (cf. the second last citation). In suffering, persons are deferred back to themselves and to what they take as the causes of their suffering. They realize what in their life is most precious to them. Hereby they find what their preferences and desires, and their dispositions are, which are frustrated.

> For, impelled by the instinct that was in him, the writer, long before he thought that one day he would become one, regularly omitted to look at a great many things which other people notice, with the result that he was accused by others of being absent-minded and by himself of not knowing how to listen or look, but all this time he was instructing his eyes and his ears to retain for ever what seemed to others puerile trivialities, the tone of voice with which a certain remark had been made, or the facial expression or the movement of the shoulders which he had seen at a certain moment, many years ago, in somebody of whom perhaps he knows nothing else what so-ever, simply be-

> cause his tone of voice was one that he had heard before or felt that he might hear again, because it was something renewable, durable. There is a feeling for generality which, in the future writer, itself picks out what is general and can for that reason one day enter into a work of art. And this has made him to listen to people only when, stupid or absurd though they may have been, they have turned themselves, by repeating like parrots what other people of similar character are in the habit of saying, into birds of augury, mouthpieces of a psychological law. He remembers only things that are general. By such tones of voice, such variations in the physiognomy, seen perhaps in his earliest childhood, has the life of other people been represented to him and when, later, he becomes a writer, it is from these observations that he composes his human figures, grafting on to a movement of the shoulders common to a number of people – a movement as truthfully delineated as though it has been recorded by an anatomist's note-book, though the truth which he uses it to express is of a psychological order – a movement of the neck made by someone else, each of many individuals having posed for a moment as his model.   (p. 937)

We see here how concept formation, i.e. generalization and association, took place in the Narrator from childhood onwards. As far as the generalization happens und perspectives that are taken in childhood and also play a role later in life, the concepts or ideas, represented by series of episodes ordered together, also order later episodes by linking them to the series with which they fit best, and are found as generalities there. These enduring perspectives are those that serve for categorizing sensations. They are kinds of tone of voice, kinds and variations of physiognomy, kinds of attitudes, kinds of emotions, kinds of form, of color, of motion, of smell, of taste, of texture, of habits, of social conduct. These are all perspectives under which low-level categories are formed and distinguished, these are not the perspectives under which ontological and intellectual categorizations are formed, which are made explicit in everyday or intellectual linguistic exchange. The following citations illustrate what the perspectives are, under which our attention to scenes and to episodes is directed, if we want to follow the Narrator.

> (It may be that, for the creation of a work of literature, imagination and sensibility are interchangeable qualities and that the latter may with no great harm be substituted for the former, ...)   (p. 937–938)

This is certainly right, since the potency of imagination is a result of previous perception and understanding. We can imagine new episodes that fit together with certain previous episodes. Neurologically, this means that we can reactivate circuits between conceptual indicators and sensory-motor and emotional systems that have previously been active. These reactivations, possibly in other combinations, result in the imaginations that can replace perceived situations as the material for the narrative content. Proust had imagined the personage of his novel in this way. He re-combined features of persons he was acquainted with in order to construct the fictive characters of his novel. They exemplify general traits of humans, which are elaborated in concrete scenes within the novel.

> The stupidest people, in their gestures, their remarks, the sentiments which they involuntarily express, manifest laws which they do not themselves perceive but which the artist surprises in them, and because he makes observations of this kind the writer is popularly believed to be ill-natured. But this belief is false: in an instance of ridiculous behaviour the artist sees a beautiful generality, and he no more condemns on this account the individual in whom he observes it than a surgeon would despise a patient for suffering from some quite common disorder... (p. 938)

> And when we seek to extract from our grief the generality that lies within it, to write about it, we are perhaps to some extent consoled for yet another reason apart from those that I have mentioned, which is that to think in terms of general truths, to write, is for the writer a wholesome and necessary function the fulfillment of which makes him happy, it does for him what is done for men of a more physical nature by exercise, perspiration, baths. (p. 939)

It seems to the Narrator that the people he writes about in his book have merely existed for the purpose of serving for him as models and as reflections for his own feelings and attitudes, and that he has profited from them as a writer.

> Saddening too was the thought that my love, to which I had clung so tenaciously, would in my book be so detached from any individual that different readers would apply it, even in detail, to what they had felt for other women. (p. 939–940)

The generalizations, laws, concepts are not part of our consciousness, but they can be shown in concrete individuals and episodes, especially in models. Thus the Narrator's love, a general disposition and typical state of mind, exemplifies itself in the several love affairs he gets involved in, and in the persons that are perceived by him as being participants in these affairs.

> And so I had to resign myself, since nothing has the power to survive unless it can become general and since the mind's own past is dead to its present consciousness, to the idea that even the people who were once most dear to the writer have in the long run done no more than pose for him like models for a painter. (p. 941)

> Thus it was that my love for Albertine, however different the two might be, was already inscribed in my love for Gilberte ... (p. 942)

> But from another point of view the work is a promise of happiness, because it shows us that in every love the particular and the general lie side by side and teaches us to pass from one to the other by a species of gymnastic which fortifies us against unhappiness by making us neglect its particular cause in order to gain a more profound understanding of its essence. (p. 942)

All this research by the Narrator into his own, and generally into any human subject's "essence", his conditions of being in the world and even creating his world, of course, makes him very self-centered, because in the Other he only wants to see what fits himself. This whole habit of investigating makes the Narrator to be finally a very lonely person. He sees himself as a product of his experiences and he sees the world, his experiences, formed by the concepts and habits he had formed by his previous experiences. He is the individual, who is forever learning, and hereby creates himself and creates for himself an evolving consciousness of the world and of other persons. By describing his world, he is directed indirectly towards himself, and towards the perceiving and acting subject generally, in its repeated acts of self-consciousness, by which he wants to find out what makes him tick, namely what makes him create his world in interaction with his surroundings. This research he does by establishing a conceptual order within his life-history, the structure that organizes all the episodes in his life, and also the episodes in some other people's lives.

8.   The home ground: Habits, routines, and general concepts

Habits are formed in memory. They are routines, i.e. generalizations over goal-directed motor activities, and thus as a kind of generalizing concepts they are part of the general memory. They are the practical analogy of experiential general concepts. Proust shows that habits are very important ordering devises in our lives. They make rooms and other places habitable, something to feel at home in, like all the familiar impressions one has of one's own room with the things one is used to. – Recall the exposition by Bergson about recognition and familiarity (Chap. 3.1). – Proust describes his bed room in Combray in detail, and a detail like the Bengal magic lantern and the projections of its scenes on the walls of the room are something unreal, but at the same time familiar. In Marcel's life the magic lantern and its projections repeatedly serve as reference point for linking scenes together which seem unreal and unusual, and are thus brought home, like the moving and changing twin steeples of Martinville he experiences when driving along the winding road. Understanding something new is integrating it into one's life-history, and it is especially seen as bringing the new experience home to the experiences of childhood. Thus the peculiar apse of Saint-Hilaire, with its asymmetrical windows high up the wall, which seems like a prison wall, serves as an unique object of his childhood to which years later he intuitively relates a similar formed high wall with such windows identifying it as "the Church", home-felt and familiar, and starting from there he remembers the childhood scenes around the church of Combray. Also other steeples remind the Narrator on the steeple of the Combray church, and are compared with it. Bringing home new experiences by connecting them to old ones and thus reviving the old ones is accompanied by a feeling of joy; it is a kind of recognition, meeting home ground, although far away from it in time and space. This home ground is rich in affections, colors, smells, tastes, what is often missing later in life, but is revived happily by activating memory via experiencing certain movements, and other bodily feelings that accidentally happen again. We also saw in the previous section how the inner life, one's own, the inner truth, or the inner reality of the general order in one's life was formed in childhood and in later life as a system of habits, dispositions, and conceptualizations on different levels of categorizing impressions, by which new situations were understood in the light of the previous ones.

Also phrases re-occur in very different matter, for example the little musical phrase by Vinteuil played by Odette for Swann and then by Albertine for Marcel, and also the phrases in Bergotte's books, which are similar by a hidden analogy. Likewise, the twin towers of Martinville were seen changing positions, forms and lights like a movement to a pretty phrase. In reading Bergotte's books similar phrases and passages merged to one "ideal passage" which cannot be described, but is felt as being typical for Bergotte's style. A style can only be experienced in its examples. This aesthetic concept of a musical phrase, or a type of literary phrase, or movement phrase is just like a general concept, or like a routine, which too is not conscious to us, but we feel its reality by experiencing the similarity while going through the different examples. This happens without being able to give a precise description of what it is that is similar. A style admits variations within undetermined margins. There is an "ideal passage", which according to the Narrator is

> common to every one of Bergotte's books, to which all the other similar passages, now becoming merged in it, had added a kind of density and volume, by which my own understanding seemed to be enlarged.   (p. 102)

As we have read in the previous section, the recognition of this similarity causes "a joy that I was experiencing in a deeper, vaster, and integrated part of myself" (p. 101). Such intellectual pleasure is an aesthetic pleasure of congruence, fitting, and slight modification of that which is familiar, and it involves sensorial as well as motor activity. Of course, also Proust's *A la recherche du temps perdu* as a whole is composed in lines of analogy and similarities with repetitions and variations.

This process of conscious, reflective recognition of examples as being instances of the same implicit concept, order, or style gives us aesthetic pleasure. The concrete is the matter in which we can experience the general. We cannot experience concepts, generalizations, ideas, styles and routines by themselves. In fact, they are nothing by themselves. They merely exist for us in their examples and can only be felt there in experiencing the similarity and the variations between the examples and feeling the pleasure of this intellectual and aesthetic activity. The concepts do not exist hidden in our mind; they rather are dispositions or capacities formed by exploring our surroundings from early childhood on. It is a natural cognitively basic process the happy result of which we feel in perceiving the examples, the episodes, as fitting into a generalizing pattern. The happiness accompanying these experiences seems to be caused by standing still at the example and realizing that it fits with the previous similar episodes encountered in our life-history that form our general concepts and routines. The previous steps of the learning process can be replayed in consciousness by remembering some of the old examples and experiencing consciously not only the commonality between the examples, but also modifications in the general pattern. Thus a new example can come to carry with it the enrichment provided by some of the old ones, which we can re-create with the help of our specific memory of episodes and individuals. It is this home ground from which we constantly create and re-create our world in understanding ourselves in interaction with our natural and social surroundings.

CHAPTER 4

Epilogue
The conscious and the unconscious

The present study, focusing on the aspects that make Proust's novel an externalization of the cognitive development of the Narrator, is largely in agreement
with Epstein (2004), who gives an account of Proust's work and his remarks
on aesthetic experience in terms of William James distinction between nucleus
and fringe, namely conscious experience and near-conscious associations that
go with it. He furthermore establishes a very rough parallel between this phenomenological side and neurological findings about brain areas involved in
remembrance. Epstein finds that Proust "Observes his memory in action, and
he uses these observations to develop a comprehensive theory of conscious experience and artistic creation that potentially has profound implications for
any scientific theory of consciousness" (2004: 214). What do we learn from his
article about this theory of conscious experience? What do we learn about artistic creation? What are the profound implications? And what is the criticism of
his account from out the perspective of the present study?

Epstein claims that voluntary recollections are just isolated snapshots of
past episodes, "which represent individual sensory events that have been abstracted from their contexts and can be recalled at will" (2004: 218), while
involuntary memories "involve recollection of an entire nexus of sensations,
thoughts, and impressions from the past" (2004: 217). The non-overt associations, "thoughts of relations" that guide a stream of thoughts or experiences
from one to the other, the "fringe" in Jamesian terms, is contextual hidden
information that contributes to the meaning of the overt thoughts or experiences, and connects them within a stream of consciousness. The sensory
experiences are in the focus, the nuclei of consciousness are connected to each
other by the hidden network of relations and associations, of which we are
merely dimly aware, or not at all (2004: 219). What happens in Proust's involuntary remembrances is, according to Epstein, that these near-conscious
relations and associations are recovered and expressed and thus are elevated
into consciousness.

I think that this picture is basically right. However, it is not complete enough to make us understand of why this expression within consciousness has an aesthetic value. Furthermore, also every perception, every remembrance, voluntary or involuntary, and every thought is embedded within a web of associations and relations, and we can make some of these explicit by asking and answering questions about the conscious experiences. With respect to an episode of drinking tea with somebody we can ask with what other persons we used to drink tea, what kind of tea we used to drink, whether we also like other kinds of tea, why we chose this kind of tea, whether the other person might have preferred coffee, whether we should have offered sugar, etc. Every aspect of the situation can lead to asking a question and by this it brings into consciousness the conceptual space, which the perspective created by the question opens up. We always need a perspective, which we take consciously or unconsciously, in order to select part of the immense network of connections that can lead to associations with an experience or action. It is not typical for involuntary memory that it recovers all this relational information. Voluntary remembrances give rise to the same. Rather the question is what kind of relational information is relevant to aesthetic experience.

For Proust it is the special sensorial character of the associations, their relationships with the emotions and sensitivities of the Narrator as a youth, and as an observant artistic person later in life. The special artistic view consists in choosing, and also in involuntarily taking perspectives, that embed an episode or situation predominantly into those series of situations and episodes, that do not represent the common concepts of daily life and orientation. In normal conceptualization or understanding of the episode it is automatically and implicitly embedded into series that represent our normal common concepts, but in the novel, the episodes are explicitly embedded into new kinds of series, into other conceptual orderings than usual. This is what also metaphoric understanding does: A situation, which first is characterized in the normal way by embedding it within the normal series of similar and also of contiguous situations created under the standard perspectives for this kind of situation, is then embedded by similarity under a new perspective into other series of situations and hereby is understood or conceptualized in a different way.

Epstein (2004: 222) remarks that in the moment which opens up the underlying memory associations we have "to separate ourselves from our current emotional context" in order to be free to observe the associations as objects in their own right. This is not quite right. Certainly we have to distance ourselves from current practical goals, and the whole current situational context, but especially bodily sensations and emotions incited with them are just what is common between the current situation and the ones that are remembered. These emotions and sensations make for the roots in reality that give the Narrator the feeling as if the remembered situation was real, and thus Time Past becomes Time Again, in which from the one remembrance a whole scene and development of scenes and surroundings of the past gets reproduced as remembrances in imagination, via the similarity and contiguity relationships that form the network of general and specific, historical, memory.

The aesthetic pleasure, the aesthetic emotions, are of another kind than the emotions and sensations that are part of the remembered episodes. The aesthetic emotions are of second order, as also Kant has observed. They are the enjoyment of ones own cognitive powers, which are the capabilities of perceiving, imagining, recognizing, conceptualizing, remembering objects and situations, and even re-living whole scenes and episodes. I think that this is understanding ourselves as understanding human beings, and thus it also is understanding what our consciousness consists of, but it is not "understanding the structure of consciousness" as "that what guides the stream of thought", as Epstein (2004:222) formulates. Consciousness consists of perceptions, images, remembrances, thoughts, speech acts, and other actions with relations between them, of which we are conscious, such that we can understand texts and larger courses of events. Consciousness is not a stream of thought, though this was a current metaphor in the first half of the 20th century. The whole constructive enterprise of Proust's novel shows the opposite of this picture.

Epstein sees Proust's novel as an expression of the associative structure of the Narrators mind within the metaphoric order of the episodes that make up the novel. That nearly is also my interpretation of the novel, except that I see the whole novel not so much as an externalization by a stream of thoughts, or by a fixed structure of underlying associations within such a stream. The novel does not have a stream-like dynamics. Rather it is more a developing system of conceptualization, a life-history of concept formation and growing understanding, whereby there is not only partial identity of aspects between similar situations and similar relationships (analogies) between situations and the behavioral and emotional reactions of the persons involved, but there is also contrast and change, and there are totally new experiences the Narrator makes, for example the horrors of the war and in parallel and contiguity with these the sado-masochistic scene in which M. Charlus participates in Jupien's hostel, which all leads to new orderings among situations, which are new conceptualizations, new ways of understanding social and individual human situations.

Epstein (2004:233), though he refers to neural networks of the different brain areas and their relationships, still sees the brain as a processing machine in which sensorial information of different modalities is processed and combined with local and conceptual information stored in other areas into a composed "representation, on which the hippocampus operates to determine the next substantive thought. Put simply: the representations that directly determine the progression of the stream of thought are not the content of consciousness." He agrees with Jackendoff in that we are not directly aware of our thoughts, only of "imagistic representations that convey the results." This last, of course, is right, but this position is still couched in a mentalist terminology that is a relict of the traditional rationalistic model of cognition, seen as embodied in a computer. A hidden mind is assumed, in which there are hidden thoughts and hidden contents that function in a process of thinking. There also is assumed a control unit that operates on such contents or representations. Also Epstein's talk about information and representations in the brain fits more with the traditional cognitive model than it does accord with the neurological model.

We should take seriously that, strictly speaking, the neurons or groups of neurons are not contents and are not representations, and that the ions transmitted across the synapses and along the axons and dendrites are not transmitted information. The activity in a neural network only has a semantic value by forming activation circuits that involve the sensory-motor areas, and via these form a referential causal connection via our body with the world around us. They indicate and point at something in the world only in referential and predicative acts of the individual. They are not information or representations by themselves. These activation circuits must be organized in a constituent structure of sub-circuits, induced from out the indices of the episodic memory and/or the short-term memory. Only with such a constituent structure, when it involves the sensory-motor areas, there is thought, which is more than just masses of associations. There are no contents without the sensory-motor areas and their relationship with the body and its surroundings. There are no hidden contents, only overt ones in consciousness.

Epstein also assumes a special area in the brain in which an aesthetic judgment is made by unconsciously comparing thoughts among each other and with current goals for fit, "thus, the conscious experience of beauty we feel when looking at a work of art may be the experiential correlate of judgments made in the frontal lobes" (2004:234). This also seems misguided. A judgment always is a conscious judgment, and of course, we may have feeling of fit, which is part of the aesthetic judgment. But the feeling of fit is not made by a judgment, but simply is the result of an activation circuit being built up with neuronal firing in some rhythm, and also by sensory-motor activity being partially embedded in it. This sensory-motor involvement creates an impression that then fits, according to our judgment. It can also induce a circuit activation resulting in a remembrance from out the partial overlap with its underlying activation circuit. The underlying neural activation circuits of an impression or a movement fit best with those conceptual and routine indicators that have been built up in the connectionist network by previous similar experiences. This fit on the neurological level can then cause the (conscious) experience of a fit in similarity or contiguity between episodes, such that we can make a judgment about this fit. This is the normal way of perceiving or understanding received sensory input. The stimuli of the new experience or movement cause activation that runs most smoothly along those connections that have been strengthened by previous similar input or motor activity. The currently undisturbed running of the activation circuit probably causes the momentary feeling of fit or recognition. This feeling of fit might indeed be part of the aesthetic judgment. But I think that that there is more to an aesthetic judgement, because this feeling of fit is part of every recognition, identification, or characterization of an object or a situation, which is fitting something new into a pattern of old experiences.

Epstein's conclusion about art is the following (2004: 236): "The goal of art is to indirectly represent these neuronal networks, which control the stream of thought but cannot themselves be directly experienced." This, I think is totally wrong: This is the goal of the neural scientist and not of art or of the artist. If we, not being neurologists or neuro-psychologists, would ever see our neural system at work, we would not take any pleasure from it, though some curiosity would be satisfied. And why should we indirectly represent it in art, and not better directly, as a scientist would do? Epstein goes on with his very last sentence: "Essentially, art is a trick that allows us to indirectly convey the structure of our minds." This sounds much better, but the problem is that there are no such (hidden) minds. Epstein makes the mistake that Bennett and Hacker (2003) criticize. He mixes up our brain or neural networks with our capacities as persons, and he assumes that there is a hidden mind consisting of hidden thoughts and, may be, also images.

Even if Proust may have assumed, with his time, that there is a hidden mind, in which the "essences" or "ideas" are established, he thinks that his novel has the task to show or represent these essences. laws, or ideas in the order of the episodes established by similarity and contiguity relationships, detectable under certain perspectives.

As we know today, there rather is the connectionist neuronal structure, which is partly fairly stable, partly changing slowly with experience, which is the physical basis of the capacity that determines our possible behavior, our possible actions, possible feelings and possible thoughts, and encompassing these, our possible forms or ways of life. These form a quite different onto-logical realm than neuronal patterns, and they are created by our interaction with our natural and social surroundings. It the realm in which we live or can imagine to live. In other words: Art tries to explore our possible worlds, as also Proust's Narrator explains to us. But there is no hidden mind, only an overt mind, namely the whole of our conscious states. And there are our possibili-ties, provided by our abilities, innate ones and acquired ones. The worlds that are possible for a subject are, semantically speaking, the extensionalizations of its capacities and abilities formed in interacting with the world, as it is and develops during the life time of a person. The exploration of our possibilities, but also, in contrast, the creation of unfitting impossibilities and absurdities, which under some perspective can have meaning, may be one prominent goal of the arts.

The theory of *Dynamic Conceptual Semantics* and *Consciousness Emerging* contains a clear description of the difference between unconscious, but cogni-tively relevant brain processes and states, dispositions and capacities of brain and body, and those brain processes and states that have consciousness emerg-ing and hereby are the neural basis of mental states and acts. This distinction, its role in intentionality, and its application to the main character of Proust's novel, the Narrator, are the last topics of this final chapter.

We distinguish three different states:

1. Conscious states, as there are states of experiencing situations (perception and imagination), own movements and own bodily states (proprioception and imagination), emotional states, and states of self-consciousness (re-flection on own conscious states), states of empathy with others (states of imagining and externally or internally imitating states that fit with the situation and expression of others).

2. Unconscious, but near-conscious states, which are circuit activations via connections between conceptual indicators in the general memory and indices in the specific memory. These states are unconscious as long as they do not involve sensorial and motor fields as part of the circuit ac-tivation and thus miss phenomenal qualities and therefore do not result in the expression of representations of situations or utterances. This can happen when other sensorial inputs and other pre-motor activity occupy

the sensorial and motor fields. We are in these kinds of states of near-perception, near-imagination, near-remembrance and near-articulation of actions when we hear, read, and understand linguistic utterances and inscriptions, without really imaging the situations described, but still have the impression that we understand what we read or hear.

3. Deep-unconscious states are our dispositions and capacities, which are based on the connectivity between conceptual indicators (the general memory, including routine indicators and indicators of emotions and bodily experiences) and indices in the specific memory. These general indicators and specific indices, and the connection strength between them, has been formed in learning processes based on previous experiences, and for some part it is possibly inherited as a bias in the course of evolution. So there seems to be an innate capacity to recognize faces, which must be due to certain strongly grown connections between certain groups of neurons in the visual system. It is known that some people have an inborn deficiency in the visual recognition of persons through their faces. One of the most basic, cognitively relevant capacities is the possibility of having organized circuit activations, which provide the ability to recognize conceptual semantic constituent structures in situations generally, and specifically in utterances. The most basic cognitively relevant capacity is the capacity to learn by establishing order and generally structures on sets of data based on similarity and contiguity.

These three categories of neurological states can be applied to the question whether Intentions (beliefs, wishes, interests, plans, goals) have as contents representations in the form of propositions, and are thus necessarily conscious states, or whether they also can be unconscious.

Intentional states can be conscious ones according to the first category of states. This means that we here have representations of the intentional contents in the form of pictures, images, perceptions, and especially in the form of perceptions, imaginations or pre-articulation states of linguistic utterances or inscriptions. This is what is assumed by philosophers in the line of Searle's (1983, 1992) writings about Intentionality. However, there also is an unconscious brand of Intentionality, namely the one that has "contents" in the form of category 2, the near-conscious states, which lack representations on the level of consciousness. Here, the intentional contents are just the circuit activations between the indicators and indices of the general and the specific memory, and are therefore not contents by themselves. They can be of influence on our actions in situations which we experience at a certain moment, if the circuit activation which carries the perception of this situation activates, via certain links, the circuit activation between the indicators and indices in the memory, without leading to being conscious of what they indicate. This happens if they cannot involve the sensorial areas because these are occupied by the perception of the present situation. The links are indicators of partly identical aspects of the present situation with previously experienced situations, which had involved certain action routines and/or certain emotions and evaluations. These can now be activated with the present situation and can cause a certain reaction. We then tend to say that this reaction was due to a hidden intention. But the content of this intention was not a proposition in a hidden mind, which does not exist. Rather it merely was a certain part of the brain activity, which potentially could be represented in imagination or pre-articulation activity, if the sensorial and motor fields were free to receive this activation from the areas of general indicators, eventually causing also an overt linguistic expression in some cases. Since the traditional use of the term 'intention' suggest that the intentional state is conscious, I would rather speak of "activated dispositions" than of unconscious intentions.

Likewise, driving a car on the freeway, while being busy with another consciously performed activity, thrives on such activated dispositions, or "unconscious" intentions. We are sensitive to information about the road, without being conscious of every relevant detail. The informational input of the road's conditions passes through the visual, and also auditory sensorial systems to the fields of conceptual and routine indicators, and from there on to the motor fields directing the automatic actions performed by the driver. A conscious perception and reaction would require a circuit activation between the sensorial fields and the conceptual indicators, and between these and the (pre-)motor fields (see also Lamme 2000, 2003 for the distinction between conscious and unconscious awareness).

Dispositions, the third category, are ways to perceive and understand situations and to act and react in them, which are not active at the moment. They are a capacity, which consists in the fact that there are certain connections between certain groups of neurons, which can be used to propagate activation and to realize activation circuits that can involve certain groups of neuron on the sensorial and motor fields, as well as on emotion and proprioception fields. Such dispositions are acquired in learning processes, or they can be innate. In principle, both work in the same way, though the innate ones are strong from the beginning and tend to stay stronger throughout the life of the individual. They are not so easily suppressed by competing activation circuits, and their suppression, when it happens, can be felt as a frustration. These dispositions are part of the deep-unconscious as long as they are not activated; then they are a mere potentiality. When they get activated, they are actual in the category of the near-conscious, in which they can stay unconscious as mere circuit activation between conceptual indicators and specific memory indices, or they can become conscious if they get represented by involving the sensorial and motor fields in the circuit activation.

Finally I want to apply the three categories to the states of the Narrator in Proust's novel. In the Section 6 of Chapter 3 above, Proust's ideas on the relationship between the conscious and the unconscious has been presented and interpreted in the light of *Dynamic Conceptual Semantics* and *Consciousness Emerging*. Proust describes how the Narrator tries to reveal the unconscious in consciousness. How far does he succeed in doing this for the two categories of the unconscious mentioned above?

The unconscious in the category of near-consciousness consists of the indicators of the concepts and routines, and the indices of the specific episodes and the connecting associations of indicators and indices of linguistic representations, namely descriptions, of long-term social and historical facts. All this forms the home-ground of the Narrator's perception and understanding of the situations he encounters. The specific historical concepts, including individual concepts, are formed by the specific episodes of his life-history, and his description of the episodes in which the other characters of the novel take part, and the individual concepts of persons and places. Historical concepts are also facts of life of social groups and the history of family clans, social groups, and nations. The general concepts and routines are based on repetition of experiences and actions, and on generalizations performed over historical concepts. Both, general concepts and routines, and specific historical concepts, determine the Narrator's and the reader's ways of perceiving and understanding new episodes, and his dealings with respect to these. Concepts are unconscious for us, and in the strict sense they do not exist. What exists is the process of formation and strengthening of a certain connectivity in the brain in the course of receiving data, which is such that the data get ordered on the basis of already existing connectivity and the connections get changed or new connection get established by incoming data that do not quite fit into the ordering established on the older data. These orderings established on the data are the concepts. They can be shown only by their results in perception and action of the characters in the novel, and especially of the Narrator. Here we can see how a present situation is understood in the light of previously experienced episodes and concepts and routines formed and activated early in childhood. From the way in which the present episode is described by the Narrator and how it is explicitly related to previous episodes we can see the working of general and historical concepts.

The unconscious, but near-conscious cognitive states of the Narrator are merely shown in their results, which are the descriptions of the episodes in the Narrator's life, and his description and understanding of the episodes around other characters in relations to previously experienced episodes. They cannot be shown directly. Representations of concepts are the series of situations that exemplify the concepts, and concepts are not more than equivalence classes of such representations. The equivalence relationship was defined in the way that two concept representations, two sets of situations, are equivalent if and only if the can be united, whereby the union still is a representation of the same concept, i.e. is a member of the same equivalence class. This means that the measure of internal similarity of all representations, and their unions, is the same.

The Narrator of the novel is presented to us in his cognitive capacity of doing the work of establishing similarity and contiguity ordering between episodes, places, buildings, persons, and their actions and reactions. In this activity of ordering and creating episodes in imagination and remembrance, and in the reflection of the Narrator on this activity, and the activity of the author and the artist in general, especially in the last chapter of the novel, "Time Regained", the deep unconscious is shown in its result. The result of this capacity is just the activity of the Narrator, which at the same time is the starting point of the Narrator's creating his life-history in an ordered fashion. The deep unconscious is the ground of this capacity, which is the whole capacity of concept formation and growing understanding by embedding new situations into the already established orderings of experiences while keeping intact their stability, or extending and modifying these orderings in order to accommodate new different experiences. With this description of the capacity corresponds as its structural biological basis the neural architecture of the learning brain with its internal structure of neurons and connections between them, partly pre-established in the evolution of the human race, and in other parts established in the history of the individual's experiencing itself and the world. Proust's novel is the life-time result of an investigation into the unconscious, as it expresses itself, or emerges, in establishing the orderings on the episodes we experience in our life, which together form our episodic consciousness. Thus, the unconscious, the connectivity structure of our general and specific memory, appears as the activity of structuring our episodic consciousness, and it is laid down as a fixation in the organization of the novel.

In the light of this manner of understanding of his work, we can think of Proust not merely as a great author, but also as a philosopher, a philosopher working in a particular style, not by formulating reasons and pro-and contra argumentations for certain positions, or creating great philosophical systems. He is a philosopher of consciousness using other means, namely the means of a literary author, the means of an artist.

References

Adams, William Howard (1984). *A Proust Souvenir*. With photographs by Paul Nadar. New York-Paris: The Vendome Press.

Bartsch, Renate (1995). *Situations, Tense, and Aspect*. Berlin-New York: Mouton de Gruyter.

Bartsch, Renate (1998). *Dynamic Conceptual Semantics. A Logico-Philosophical Investigation into Concept Formation and Understanding*. Stanford, CA: CSLI.

Bartsch, Renate (2002a). *Consciousness Emerging. The Dynamics of Perception, Imagination, Action, Memory, Thought and Language*. Amsterdam-Philadelphia: John Benjamins Publishing Company.

Bartsch, Renate (2002b). Generating polysemy: Metaphor and metonymy. In R. Dirven & R. Pörings (Eds.), *Metaphor and Metonymy in Comparison and Contrast* (pp. 49–74). Berlin-New York: Mouton de Gruyter.

Bennett, M. R. & Hacker, P. M. S. (2003). *Philosophical Foundations of Neuroscience*. Oxford: Blackwell.

Bergson, Henri (1908). Materie und Gedächtnis. *Essays zur Beziehung zwischen Körper und Geist* (Transl. by Wilhelm Windelband). Jena: Eugen Diederichs.

Brouwer, Elsbeth (2003). *Imagining Metaphors. Cognitive Representation in Interpretation and Understanding*. Amsterdam: ILLC, University of Amsterdam.

Chomsky, Noam (1995). Language and nature. *Mind, 104*(413), 1–62.

Conway, Martin, M. (2001). Sensory-perceptual episodic memory and its context: autobiographical memory. *Transactions of the Royal Academy London B, 356*, 1375–1384.

Conway, Martin M. & Pleydell-Peirce, Christopher W. (2000). The construction of autobiographical memories in the self-memory system. *Psychological Review, 107*, 261–288.

Damasio, Antonio R. (1999). *The Feeling of What Happens*. New York: Harcourt Brace.

Dalatour, B. & Witter, M. P. (2002). Projections from the parahippocampal region to the prefrontal cortex in the rat: Evidence of multiple pathways. *European Journal of Neuroscience, 15*(8), 1400–1407.

Davidson, Donald (1980[1967]). The logical form of action sentences. *Essays on Actions and Events* (pp. 105–148). Oxford: Clarendon Press.

Davidson, Donald (1985). *Inquiries into Truth and Interpretation*. Oxford: Clarendon Press.

Draaisma, Douwe (2001). *Waarom het leven sneller gaat als je ouder wordt. Over het autobiographische geheugen*. [Why time goes faster when we get old: About autobiographic memory]. Groningen: Historische Uitgeverij.

Epstein, Russell (2004). Consciousness, art, and the brain: Lessons from Marcel Proust. *Consciousness and Cognition, 13*, 213–240.

Haberlandt, Karl (1999). *Human Memory. Exploration and Application.* Boston, London: Allyn and Bacon.

Hasselmo, M. E., Bodelon, C., & Wyble, B. P. (2002). A proposed function for hippocampal theta rhythm: Separate phases of encoding and retrieval enhance reversal of prior learning. *Neural Computation, 14*, 793–817.

Hasselmo, M. E., Hay, J., Ilyn, M., & Gorchetchnikov, A. (2002). Neuromodulation, theta rhythm and rat spatial navigation. *Neural Networks, 15*, 689–707.

Hasselmo, M. E., Cannon, R. C., & Koene, R. A. (2002). A simulation of parahippocampal and hippocampal structures guiding spatial navigation of a virtual rat in a virtual environment. A functional framework for theta theory. In M. P. Witter & F. G. Wouterlood (Eds.), 139–161.

Husserl, Edmund (1985[1939]). *Erfahrung und Urteil.* Hamburg: Felix Meiner Verlag.

Jackendoff, Ray (2002). *Foundations of Language: Brain, Meaning, Grammar, Evolution.* Oxford: Oxford University Press.

Lamme, Victor A. F. (2000). Neural mechanisms of visual awareness: A linking proposition. *Brain and Mind, 1*, 385–406.

Lamme, Victor A. F. & Roelfsema, P. R. (2000). The distinct modes of vision offered by feed-forward and recurrent processing. *Trends in Neurosciences, 23*, 571–579.

Lamme, Victor A. F. (2002). Masking interrupts figure-ground signals in 1. *Journal of Cognitive Neuroscience, 14*, 1–10.

Lamme, Victor A. F. (2003). Why visual attention and awareness are different. *Trends in Cognitive Sciences, 7*, 12–18.

Miyashita, Yasushi (2004). Cognitive memory: Cellular and network machineries and their top-down control. *Science, 306*, 435–440.

Morris, Richard G. M. (2003). Memory and the hippocampus: Elements of a neuro-biological theory (Lecture at the CSCA Symposium: In search of memory traces. Amsterdam July 7, 2004, based on a talk at the Royal Society in May 2003). *Philosophical Transactions of the Royal Society, 358*, 7773–7786.

Neisser, Ulric & Fivush, Robin (Eds.). (1994). *The Remembering Self. Construction and Accuracy in the Self-Narrative.* Cambridge: Cambridge University Press.

Painter, George D. (1983[1959]). *Marcel Proust. A Biography.* Harmondsworth: Penguin Books.

Peacocke, Ch. (1992). *A Study of Concepts.* Cambridge, MA: MIT Press.

Proust, Marcel (1981). *Remembrance of Things Past*, Volumes 1–3. (Translated by C. K. Scott Moncrieff & Terence Kilmartin from *A la recherche du temps perdu.*) Harmondsworth: Penguin Books.

Quine, W. V. O. (1960). *Word and Object.* Cambridge, MA: The MIT Press.

Quine, W. V. O. (1963). Two dogmas of empiricism. *From a Logical Point of View. Logico-Philosophical Essays* (pp. 20–46). New York: Harper and Row.

Quine, W. V. O. (1974). *The Roots of Reference.* La Salle: Open Court.

Raffone, Antonio & Wolters, Gezinus (2001). A cortical mechanism for binding in visual working memory. *Journal of Cognitive Neurociene, 13*(6), 766–785.

Rosch, Eleanor (1973). On the internal structure of perceptual and semantic categories. In T. E. Moore (Ed.), *Cognitive Development and the Acquisition of Language* (pp. 11–144). New York: Academic Press.

Rosch, Eleanor (1978). Principles of categorization. In E. Rosch & B. Lloyd (Eds.), *Cognition and Categorization* (pp. 27–48). Hilldsdale, NJ: Erlbaum.

Ryle, Gilbert (1949). *The Concept of Mind.* New York: Barnes and Noble.

Searle, John (1983). *Intentionality.* Cambridge: Cambridge University Press.

Searle, John (1992). *The Rediscovery of Mind.* Cambridge, MA: MIT Press.

Squire, Larry R. & Kandel, Eric R. (2000). *Memory – From mind to molecules.* New York: Scientific American Library, a Division of HPHLP.

Tadié, Jean-Yves (2001[1936]). *Marcel Proust – A Life.* (Transl. by Euan Cameron). New York: Penguin Books.

Wagenaar, Willem A. (1986). My Memory: A study of autobiographical memory over six years. *Cognitive Psychology, 18,* 225–252.

Winograd, Eugene & Neisser, Ulric (Eds.). (1992). *Affect and Accuracy in Recall. Studies of "flashbulb" Memories.* Cambridge: Cambridge University Press.

Witter, M. P., Groenewegen, H. J., Lohman, A. H. M., & Lopes da Silva, F. H. (1989). Functional organization of the extrinsic and intrinsic circuitry of the parahippocampal region. *Progress in Neuroscience, 33,* 161–254.

Witter, M. P. & Wouterlood, F. G. (Eds.). (2002). *The Parahippocampal Region: Organization and Role in Cognitive Functions.* Oxford: Oxford University Press.

Wittgenstein, Ludwig (1960). *Philosophische Untersuchungen.* Schriften. Frankfurt: Suhrkamp Verlag.

Index

In the series *Advances in Consciousness Research* the following titles have been published thus far or are scheduled for publication:

4   HARDCASTLE, Valerie Gray: Locating Consciousness. 1995. xviii, 266 pp.

5   STUBENBERG, Leopold: Consciousness and Qualia. 1998. x, 368 pp.

6   GENNARO, Rocco J.: Consciousness and Self-Consciousness. A defense of the higher-order thought theory of consciousness. 1996. x, 220 pp.

7   MAC CORMAC, Earl and Maxim I. STAMENOV (eds.): Fractals of Brain, Fractals of Mind. In search of a symmetry bond. 1996. x, 359 pp.

8   GROSSENBACHER, Peter G. (ed.): Finding Consciousness in the Brain. A neurocognitive approach. 2001. xvi, 326 pp.

9   Ó NUALLÁIN, Seán, Paul Mc KEVITT and Eoghan Mac AOGÁIN (eds.): Two Sciences of Mind. Readings in cognitive science and consciousness. 1997. xii, 490 pp.

10   NEWTON, Natika: Foundations of Understanding. 1996. x, 211 pp.

11   PYLKKÖ, Pauli: The Aconceptual Mind. Heideggerian themes in holistic naturalism. 1998. xxvi, 297 pp.

12   STAMENOV, Maxim I. (ed.): Language Structure, Discourse and the Access to Consciousness. 1997. xii, 364 pp.

13   VELMANS, Max (ed.): Investigating Phenomenal Consciousness. New methodologies and maps. 2000. xii, 381 pp.

14   SHEETS-JOHNSTONE, Maxine: The Primacy of Movement. 1999. xxxiv, 584 pp.

15   CHALLIS, Bradford H. and Boris M. VELICHKOVSKY (eds.): Stratification in Cognition and Consciousness. 1999. viii, 293 pp.

16   ELLIS, Ralph D. and Natika NEWTON (eds.): The Caldron of Consciousness. Motivation, affect and self-organization — An anthology. 2000. xxii, 276 pp.

17   HUTTO, Daniel D.: The Presence of Mind. 1999. xiv, 252 pp.

18   PALMER, Gary B. and Debra J. OCCHI (eds.): Languages of Sentiment. Cultural constructions of emotional substrates. 1999. vi, 272 pp.

19   DAUTENHAHN, Kerstin (ed.): Human Cognition and Social Agent Technology. 2000. xxiv, 448 pp.

20   KUNZENDORF, Robert G. and Benjamin WALLACE (eds.): Individual Differences in Conscious Experience. 2000. xii, 412 pp.

21   HUTTO, Daniel D.: Beyond Physicalism. 2000. xvi, 306 pp.

22   ROSSETTI, Yves and Antti REVONSUO (eds.): Beyond Dissociation. Interaction between dissociated implicit and explicit processing. 2000. x, 372 pp.

23   ZAHAVI, Dan (ed.): Exploring the Self. Philosophical and psychopathological perspectives on self-experience. 2000. viii, 301 pp.

24   ROVEE-COLLIER, Carolyn, Harlene HAYNE and Michael COLOMBO: The Development of Implicit and Explicit Memory. 2000. x, 324 pp.

25   BACHMANN, Talis: Microgenetic Approach to the Conscious Mind. 2000. xiv, 300 pp.

26   Ó NUALLÁIN, Seán (ed.): Spatial Cognition. Foundations and applications. 2000. xvi, 366 pp.

27   GILLETT, Grant R. and John McMILLAN: Consciousness and Intentionality. 2001. x, 265 pp.

28   ZACHAR, Peter: Psychological Concepts and Biological Psychiatry. A philosophical analysis. 2000. xx, 342 pp.

29   VAN LOOCKE, Philip (ed.): The Physical Nature of Consciousness. 2001. viii, 321 pp.

30   BROOK, Andrew and Richard C. DEVIDI (eds.): Self-Reference and Self-Awareness. 2001. viii, 277 pp.

31   RAKOVER, Sam S. and Baruch CAHLON: Face Recognition. Cognitive and computational processes. 2001. x, 306 pp.

32   VITIELLO, Giuseppe: My Double Unveiled. The dissipative quantum model of brain. 2001. xvi, 163 pp.

33 YASUE, Kunio, Mari JIBU and Tarcisio DELLA SENTA (eds.): No Matter, Never Mind. Proceedings of Toward a Science of Consciousness: Fundamental approaches, Tokyo 1999. 2002. xvi, 391 pp.

34 FETZER, James H. (ed.): Consciousness Evolving. 2002. xx, 253 pp.

35 Mc KEVITT, Paul, Seán Ó NUALLÁIN and Conn MULVIHILL (eds.): Language, Vision and Music. Selected papers from the 8th International Workshop on the Cognitive Science of Natural Language Processing, Galway, 1999. 2002. xii, 433 pp.

36 PERRY, Elaine, Heather ASHTON and Allan H. YOUNG (eds.): Neurochemistry of Consciousness. Neurotransmitters in mind. With a foreword by Susan Greenfield. 2002. xii, 344 pp.

37 PYLKKÄNEN, Paavo and Tere VADÉN (eds.): Dimensions of Conscious Experience. 2001. xiv, 209 pp.

38 SALZARULO, Piero and Gianluca FICCA (eds.): Awakening and Sleep–Wake Cycle Across Development. 2002. vi, 283 pp.

39 BARTSCH, Renate: Consciousness Emerging. The dynamics of perception, imagination, action, memory, thought, and language. 2002. x, 258 pp.

40 MANDLER, George: Consciousness Recovered. Psychological functions and origins of conscious thought. 2002. xii, 142 pp.

41 ALBERTAZZI, Liliana (ed.): Unfolding Perceptual Continua. 2002. vi, 296 pp.

42 STAMENOV, Maxim I. and Vittorio GALLESE (eds.): Mirror Neurons and the Evolution of Brain and Language. 2002. viii, 392 pp.

43 DEPRAZ, Nathalie, Francisco J. VARELA and Pierre VERMERSCH: On Becoming Aware. A pragmatics of experiencing. 2003. viii, 283 pp.

44 MOORE, Simon C. and Mike OAKSFORD (eds.): Emotional Cognition. From brain to behaviour. 2002. vi, 350 pp.

45 DOKIC, Jérôme and Joëlle PROUST (eds.): Simulation and Knowledge of Action. 2002. xxii, 271 pp.

46 MATEAS, Michael and Phoebe SENGERS (eds.): Narrative Intelligence. 2003. viii, 342 pp.

47 COOK, Norman D.: Tone of Voice and Mind. The connections between intonation, emotion, cognition and consciousness. 2002. x, 293 pp.

48 JIMÉNEZ, Luis (ed.): Attention and Implicit Learning. 2003. x, 385 pp.

49 OSAKA, Naoyuki (ed.): Neural Basis of Consciousness. 2003. viii, 227 pp.

50 GLOBUS, Gordon G.: Quantum Closures and Disclosures. Thinking-together postphenomenology and quantum brain dynamics. 2003. xxii, 200 pp.

51 DROEGE, Paula: Caging the Beast. A theory of sensory consciousness. 2003. x, 183 pp.

52 NORTHOFF, Georg: Philosophy of the Brain. The brain problem. 2004. x, 433 pp.

53 HATWELL, Yvette, Arlette STRERI and Edouard GENTAZ (eds.): Touching for Knowing. Cognitive psychology of haptic manual perception. 2003. x, 322 pp.

54 BEAUREGARD, Mario (ed.): Consciousness, Emotional Self-Regulation and the Brain. 2004. xii, 294 pp.

55 PERUZZI, Alberto (ed.): Mind and Causality. 2004. xiv, 235 pp.

56 GENNARO, Rocco J. (ed.): Higher-Order Theories of Consciousness. An Anthology. 2004. xii, 371 pp.

57 WILDGEN, Wolfgang: The Evolution of Human Language. Scenarios, principles, and cultural dynamics. 2004. xii, 240 pp.

58 GLOBUS, Gordon G., Karl H. PRIBRAM and Giuseppe VITIELLO (eds.): Brain and Being. At the boundary between science, philosophy, language and arts. 2004. xii, 350 pp.

59 ZAHAVI, Dan, Thor GRÜNBAUM and Josef PARNAS (eds.): The Structure and Development of Self-Consciousness. Interdisciplinary perspectives. 2004. xiv, 162 pp.

60 DIETRICH, Eric and Valerie Gray HARDCASTLE: Sisyphus's Boulder. Consciousness and the limits of the knowable. 2005. xii, 136 pp.

61 ELLIS, Ralph D.: Curious Emotions. Roots of consciousness and personality in motivated action. 2005. viii, 240 pp.

62 DE PREESTER, Helena and Veroniek KNOCKAERT (eds.): Body Image and Body Schema. Interdisciplinary perspectives on the body. ix, 327 pp. + index. *Expected July 2005*

63 BARTSCH, Renate: Memory and Understanding. Concept formation in Proust's *A la recherche du temps perdu*. 2005. ix, 158 pp.